8/15/13

HANDS-ON
ARCHAEOLOGY

HANDS-ON ARCHAEOLOGY

Real-Life Activities for Kids

by John R. White, Ph.D.

PRUFROCK PRESS INC.

WACO, TEXAS

©2005, John R. White

Illustrations by Kalita Alberts

Library of Congress Cataloging-in-Publication Data

White, John R. (John Robert), 1937-
     Hands-on archaeology : real-life activities for kids 9 / by John R. White.
          p. cm.
     Includes bibliographical references.
     ISBN 1-59363-162-6 (pbk.)
     1. Archaeology--Study and teaching--Activity programs. I. Title.
     CC83.W48 2005
     930.1'071'2--dc22   2005018426

Printed in the United States of America.

PRUFROCK PRESS INC.
P.O. Box 8813,
Waco, TX 76714-8813
(800) 998-2208 Fax (800) 240-0333
http://www.prufrock.com

Table of Contents

INTRODUCTION

There were three principal goals in the writing of this book:

☞ to provide elementary and secondary school teachers with an accurate and readable guide to teaching a discipline seldom, if ever, seen in pre-university curricula, but guaranteed, nonetheless, to kindle the fires of enthusiasm under young students;

☞ to allow students themselves the opportunity to join firsthand in the practice of a genuine science and, thereby, learn to appreciate the variety of skills and the magnitude of the labor that goes into the collection of such data; and finally, and most importantly,

☞ to inculcate in the minds of the youngsters an appreciation of the fragility of the archaeological record and at the same time make them aware of their roles as potential "stewards of the past."

Preservation of sites, which are in truth nonrenewable resources, is a difficult task in the best of circumstances. Knowing that there is a growing group of young people keenly aware of what archaeology's role is in the process should be encouraging to professional archaeologists, historians, preservationists, and conservationists alike.

GENESIS

This book was inevitable; it was only a matter of time. Actually, if the truth be known, it is probably a little late in arriving. More than 20 years of teaching archaeology to youngsters in primary and secondary schools has culminated in this manual. The more I interacted with students and their teachers, the more I came to realize the great potential archaeology had, not only as a motivational tool for youngsters and as a discipline capable of instructing them in a wide variety of skills, but also as an instrument for simultaneously imbuing them with an appreciation of the importance of preserving our precious cultural past.

Why Archaeology

Archaeology is an excellent tool for turning on the minds of young people in grades K–12. It can be made an integral part of the curricula of gifted programs, as well as effectively used to enhance standard education courses. It can be utilized to ignite the so often hidden curiosity of students who have difficulty working up an interest in anything scholastic. In short, it has something for everyone. But why? Such asseverations demand support. What makes archaeology so special? Why should you, as an elementary or secondary school teacher, take the time to acquaint yourself with it? I'll tell you.

Archaeology is exciting. Archaeology, as a discipline, enjoyed a renaissance of sorts in 1981 when the world was introduced to Indiana Jones. His heart-pounding adventures in search of the lost ark of the covenant led young and old alike to rethink this arcane discipline. All this despite the fact that Indiana never as much as touched a shovel. But this is not real, you say; archaeology isn't chasing after treasures or lost cities. No, certainly not, but it isn't the reality that is so important—it's the perception. There's a certain romance in seeking after the unknown. Whether a fabled city or just an ordinary tract of land that blankets an older home site or building, the allure is still there. The attraction is not in the "treasure" per se. It never was. It's the excitement of uncovering the unknown—the same thrill that comes just prior to opening that beautifully wrapped Christmas present. Remember how even the revelation of the ultimate gift was not quite as thrilling as that moment of expectation just preceding it? That is the kind of excitement archaeology dispenses—to students and teachers alike.

Few things rival the feeling of approaching a potential site—any site—for the first time. You can only wonder what the grass or weeds and the thin mantle of soil might hide. Teachers, of course, share the excitement with their youngsters, but because the students are younger than their teachers, everything in the site is "old." Find a bottle from the 1950s, and to students, it's "really old." You don't have to find a minted Roman coin dating from the age of Augustus; a 1960 penny will do quite nicely.

Archaeology is a natural. Not only is the fieldwork itself exciting, but so also are the follow-up procedures, such as the in-class cataloging, analysis, and interpretational phases. Kids, for the most part, like to be pushed intellectually, especially if the pushing looks so much like a game or puzzle. And that's a large part of what archaeology is—an often complex but always exciting puzzle for the mind. Imaginative teachers can always find innovative ways to enhance even more the "excitement quotient" of archaeology.

Archaeology is also academically and intellectually holistic. Though as a discipline it is greater than the sum of its parts, the act of caring for the various "parts" touches on a multitude of other disciplines and calls on a wide spectrum of skills. To paraphrase the words of the old song, it teaches "a little bit about a lot of things." It would take a lot more space than we have here to enumerate the intellectual advantages of such an undertaking. Suffice it to say that the young archaeologists will be making continuous deposits into at least three primary intellectual "banks"—disciplinary skills, social skills, and conceptual skills.

At the disciplinary level, and on an almost continuous basis, the youngsters work with:

Math: Mapping; laying out and gridding the site; plotting range and bearing to each artifact from datum; using compasses and surveying equipment; converting back and forth between the British system and metric.

Biology: Learning to identify various bones and the animals from which they came; recording the plants and trees associated with the site.

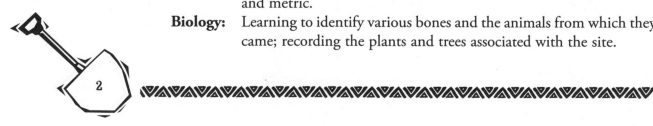

Geology:	Familiarizing oneself with the principles of site stratigraphy; learning to recognize various rocks and minerals that occur in the site.
Art:	Taking black-and-white photographs and color slides; drawing and sketching artifacts and features on the site forms; making detailed drawings of certain artifacts for display purposes; recognizing various architectural features that are uncovered; preparing museum exhibits.
Geography:	Learning to translate and use the various maps and charts utilized by archaeologists.
History:	Doing the preliminary research on the site to be dug; collecting oral histories of people familiar with the site; researching the uses of recovered historic artifacts; reading about related historical sites.
Language Skills:	Recording the field notes; writing the final report; composing accurate labels for the artifacts displays; developing vocabulary; giving oral presentations to various groups about the work.
Motor Skills:	Correctly manipulating shovels, trowels, and other digging and recording equipment.

The *social skills* are primarily derived from the team effort necessitated by such an ambitious project as a site excavation and analysis. Pulling off the job successfully takes a great deal of coordination and cooperation. Each individual, while dutifully involved with an activity to which he or she is intellectually attached, must keep in mind that the ultimate goal is the successful creation of a cohesive whole. Learning that some intellectual efforts are truly greater than the sum of their parts (even when the "part" is something you have been laboring so hard on) is a valuable lesson. It is just as important to teach youngsters how to successfully interact as it is to teach them the details of their interactions. Working on such a large-scale (and adult) project as an excavation serves to drive home the point.

Conceptual skills are those involving the ability to mentally formulate and process ideas and abstractions, part of which is learning how to utilize data in imaginative and innovative ways. More than the mere collecting of raw data, they involve, among other things, learning to look at things from an unusual perspective. For instance, carefully measuring the bearing and distances of minute stone flakes from each other and from a selected datum point teaches mathematical, or more specifically, surveying skills; but translating those measurements into an understanding of what caused the stone flakes to reach those specific locations takes thought processes of a higher level.

Here is a real example of such a learning experience that occurred during the construction of a fake mound that we intended for use in training youngsters enrolled at our archaeology camp. We used youngsters (who would not be involved in its subsequent excavation) to build the mound and place its contents. Mary L., a bright 11-year-old, sat cross-legged on a small flat rock and carefully knocked flint flakes from a cobble core in an attempt to make a crude stone chopper. She, a southpaw, carefully noted where her popped-off flakes were landing. When she turned the job over to Bob

T., a right-hander, she noted a different scatter pattern resulting from his work. "Dr. White, maybe we can tell whether an Indian who left flakes behind was left- or right-handed."

Maybe we can! This is a genuine intellectual insight. This is the stuff of which great archaeologists and detectives are made. Most of all, it is the stuff that really exercises young minds. And it happens all the time on archaeological excavations!

Teachers can stretch and expand—or reduce—any part of the archaeological experience to suit their own pedagogical needs. A history course can emphasize the historical research; the math teacher, the measurements and mensuration involved; the art teacher, the drawing, photography, and museum display; the social studies teacher, the archaeology itself; and on and on. The teaching of archaeology is limitless in its potential. Teachers can expand into areas where they have special expertise or into which they want their young charges to go. In short, archaeology is multiplicitous; it has something for everyone.

Archaeology is innovative. It offers the opportunity to both teachers and students to break away from the traditional four-walled classroom and to substitute the fresh air and invigorating atmosphere of the out-of-doors. While change by itself is not necessarily an advantage, there is something to be gained by a change that gives young people the opportunity to gather original data firsthand rather than from books. While not dispensing entirely with traditional pedagogical methods, archaeology does allow for the inclusion of learning experiences just not available within the confines of the school walls.

What child doesn't like the idea of getting his or her hands dirty in the pursuit of some perceived "treasure"? Who wouldn't rather learn about plants or minerals or bones by collecting genuine specimens in the field rather than merely checking out pictures in a book? And finally, who amongst us doesn't agree that a big gulp of fresh air taken under a sunny sky helps to clear the learning "sinuses" and make the educational experience a much more refreshing one?

Archaeology isn't just exciting to the participants; everyone enjoys it. Archaeology has the advantage over almost every other discipline (even at the college level) in that it is quite visual. Television stations and newspapers fall all over themselves to cover site excavations. It does not matter that it's just a bunch of youngsters digging on an abandoned lot. Archaeology is visual and the camera loves it! It captures people and personalities, but most of all it captures movement and action. Let me tell you why this is important.

In my considerable experience working with elementary and secondary school children ranging in age from 10 to 18, I have never failed to get evening news coverage after only one phone call to a local news station. In some cases, local TV stations have run series on our work. The same thing that makes archaeology so popular with network producers who scatter the evening airwaves with one-hour archaeology specials such as "NOVA," and "National Geographic" on channels like Odyssey and Discovery makes it popular with local news directors. It has a built-in audience.

Don't underestimate the value of archaeology's ability to draw attention to your school. In a day when the public tends to be in a castigatory mood with respect to our school systems, a nice piece on the six o'clock news helps to square the balance. *Principals love good public relations.*

Use the public relations engendered by your little dig to increase interest in local history, your school, and the educational system in general. Your own stock with your school administrators will positively soar!

Past Experiences and Successes

From a personal standpoint, my own experience working with young people (of less than college age) goes back to 1975. A phone call I received in the spring of that year came from a social studies teacher in the Struthers (a suburb of Youngstown, OH) school system who inquired whether it would be possible to use high school seniors in the excavation of an archaeological site. His query was prompted by a newly funded grant proposal, the Struthers Total Environmental Education Program (STEEP). In it, standard high school disciplines were to be taught outside the classroom—hence the phrase "Total Environmental Education." He thought history could be taught as historical archaeology, thereby giving the students a rare hands-on opportunity. I agreed wholeheartedly.

Over the next two summers, my small crew, the high school students, and I completely uncovered the stone remains of the historic Eaton (Hopewell) blast furnace. Built in 1802—the earliest blast furnace of any kind west of the Allegheny Mountains and later determined by our own post-seasonal analyses to be the earliest in the New World to use coal in combination with charcoal as a fuel—the Eaton was subsequently placed on the National Register of Historic Places. There was nothing contrived about it. The success of the excavation depended to a large degree on the labors and skills of the student diggers. Can you imagine the thrill of being part of such an effort?

It was in 1980 that my next contact with young archaeologists came about. In that year we were carrying out important excavations for the state of Ohio of a historic tavern site dating from the post-Revolutionary War period. The site just happened to be located on the 600-plus acre summer camp property belonging to the Dayton YMCA. Needless to say, we spent a good portion of our time answering questions posed by the campers who were hiking near our dig in the course of each day. Eventually it became such a "problem" that we decided to enlist one of our crew as an official tour guide. Interest continued to grow, and by the close of our dig season, we actually had a "minidig" set aside for the campers and their counselors.

The next year, the official tavern dig completed, I approached the outdoor education director with a proposition: Supply me and my crew with room and board at the camp and permission to dig—I wanted very much to seriously explore the prehistoric potential in the camp area as it sits in the shadow of monumental Fort Ancient—and we would allow a select number of young campers (11 to 16 years of age) to dig side by side with us on a genuine dig. As the Godfather would say, "It was an offer they could not refuse." That is how the first camp of its kind was started in southern Ohio in 1981. It turned out to be immensely successful by every standard.

Every year since then, 75 youngsters, split almost evenly between girls and boys, have attended camp—in one-week sessions of 25 each—and in the process have actively participated in the discovery and excavation of two 75-foot-long prehistoric stone snakes that are now on the National Register of Historic Places. Some of these early participants still keep in touch.

In 1986, Youngstown State University began its participation in the Governor's Institute program. In the first year of university involvement, archaeology was the only discipline participating. It was chosen as the showcase for some of the same reasons that elementary and secondary school teachers should be attracted to it. It was seen as exciting, unusual, and telegenic. Even with all of its intellectual worth, archaeology's ability to draw good PR was viewed as a bonus.

In the first season, my crew of three field assistants and I had more than 100 diggers. It was absolute bedlam! It amounted to nothing more than an exercise in crowd control. No one, anywhere, would ever attempt excavations with a gang this large—even if they were all professionals. It would be tantamount to having 60 surgeons trying earnestly to get to your appendix. So the first year was more of a learning experience for us than for the students. We knew the basic idea was sound, however, and the next year we arranged the dig so that it was broken up into smaller groups extending over a longer period of time. Still, some kinks remained. By the fourth year, we had it running like clockwork and were serving 100-plus 10th- and 11th-graders from northeastern Ohio and giving them a wonderful taste of real archaeology. The program is now in its 12th year, still immensely popular—it is the first of the university courses to close its rolls—and still saturating young people with fresh air and fresh ideas. And it hasn't stopped there.

Even as I write this introduction, my mind is on the two high school archaeology programs that have just been initiated locally and for which I serve as a consultant. The work is never-ending—and so rewarding. Nothing succeeds like success.

Why the Book?

This book was a natural next step in the evolutionary process which began when we undertook teaching those young campers how to increase their appreciation of the past, while simultaneously attending to their education in a wide range of disciplines. Initially, we could "fly by the seat of our pants," teaching as we went, so to speak.

We soon realized, however, that there was more to education than simply having a good time with it. There were responsibilities that had to be met. First, we had a responsibility to the student. We wanted to make the archaeological experience fulfilling in the literal sense. This meant doing all (or at least most) of the things that professional archaeologists do at a site (and do afterward) and doing them as faithfully as age and experience would allow. This goal of covering such a variety of tasks would also help ensure that a complete spectrum of disciplinary skills was taught. At the same time that youngsters were learning the prerequisite archaeological skills, we would be doing incidental justice to the site by retrieving the data as accurately as possible. In order to accomplish this goal, more was required than a mere outline of tasks. A manual, of sorts, was sorely needed.

An article written for and published by *Gifted Child Today Magazine* in 1995 listed the steps necessary for the excavation of an "empty lot" site. If the number of calls I received for reprints or for follow-up information was any indication, the article was well read. It was the requests for more details that convinced me that the bare-bones article had to be fleshed out with more specifics—and with more precautionary notes. What was needed was a detailed description of just what to do during each phase of a successful dig, along with a series of ironclad rules that would serve as the Mosaic Code for the teachers/archaeologists, an explanation and glossary of technical terms in common archaeological use, and a series of activities that could be used to supplement the archaeological fieldwork. In short, we needed a book.

You will note, as you read, that the text is interrupted occasionally by the word "activity" followed by a number (📙 **Activity #1** 📙). These activity "pauses" indicate points at which teachers might wish to drop in one of the numbered activities found at the end of each chapter. The activities are placed to coincide with what's going on in the classroom. Though carefully chosen to enhance the various aspects of archaeology being discussed, there might well be compelling reasons for adding to, subtracting from, or totally ignoring any one of them. Feel free to do so. This is your manual. Use it in the way that it works best *for you*.

TAKING CARE OF ESSENTIALS

Field archaeology—as opposed to in-the-classroom archaeology—can be taught at the elementary, secondary, or university level in one of three ways: digging a genuine archaeological site (either historical or prehistoric), constructing and digging an artificial site or mound, or excavating an empty lot. A few distinctions have to be made. Although listed as an alternative, the use of a genuine site is *not* a choice for pre-university-level students, or for that matter, anyone not being directed by a trained archaeologist. Genuine sites are unique, nonrenewable resources that, under *no* circumstances, should ever be excavated with anything but the greatest care and by individuals whose primary interest is the accurate retrieval of too easily lost data.

While it is true that instructing archaeology students at the university level does necessitate using untrained personnel to dig often-valuable sites, the Society for American Archaeology ethics committee requires that instruction never be the primary reason for digging the site, rather it must always be ancillary to accurate data removal and site preservation. Let's use a parallel from a modern hospital. Interns (doctors-in-training or advanced medical students) are used in the performance of real operations (it is the only way they can learn to do surgery), but their on-the-job training, as important as it may be, always takes a backseat to the welfare of the patient. Trained surgeons move in when and if the need arises. Archaeologists treat their sites with much the same deference. So, the genuine site is out. What then? Well, we can always build our own site.

It has been shown time and again that a site, or "mound," can be constructed from scratch and, thereby, assure that it contains the required range of artifacts and archaeological "problems." Such artificial mounds and the discussion of their construction and instructional effectiveness have been written about elsewhere; not everyone, however, can afford the time and expense of constructing such an elaborate instructional device. Fortunately there is a viable alternative: use the empty lot of a recently razed structure.

Choosing the Site

Empty lots abound in both urban and rural areas, and so there is usually one to be found near every school. Urban renewal and expansion of people and businesses into the suburbs assures us of a steady supply of such sites. Okay, so the site is readily available; what next? How do we turn a barren lot into a classroom? Of course, before you do anything else you must get *informed* permission from the lot owner. Getting informed consent means telling the owner specifically what you intend to do. The clearer you are on this the more likely you are to get quick support. This usually includes liability guarantees and assurances that you will return the property to essentially the same state it was in before you began work. This means backfilling the holes you have dug and leveling the ground. Such things are not done only for cosmetic purposes but also to remove potential hazards created by ardent diggers. My first professional prehistoric dig consisted of initially convincing a very hesitant California cattle rancher that we would leave behind no deep excavations—"tank traps" as he called them—for his prize heifers to fall into. Having convinced the landowner that you will perform such corrective duties—and in the process hinted of the very favorable publicity likely to befall an individual who contributes so generously to the support of public education—you are ready to begin converting your grassy or weed-covered tract into a schoolroom.

One word of caution. It must be understood that the only difference between the genuine site and the usable empty lot is the perceived significance of one over the other. In truth, both are, by definition, archaeological sites; the difference lies in the fact that in one case there is information below ground that is in need of more careful handling than the other. But this is all relative; both sites must be dug with seriousness and due care. The advantage of the empty lot, and the reason why it is the ideal choice at the pre-university level, is in its "forgiveness" of error and youthful mishap.

> Ironclad Rule #1—Always check with a professional archaeologist to ensure that the empty lot is not a site whose importance or potential significance would require professional handling. Do not excavate before checking with an archaeologist or other expert. This is the single most important rule of them all.

Building Your Resource Library

Like anyone starting out on a long trip through unfamiliar terrain, you will want to acquaint yourself with certain basic data which you can consider road signs to a successful arrival at your destination. While it might be exaggerating to say that resources abound in the area of archaeology in the pre-university curricula, still there are a fair number of materials available in the form of newsletters, articles, texts, workbooks, activity center kits, curricular guides, simulation games, and computer software. Many of them are free for the asking.

Teachers will want to include in their resource library some things that are of particular interest to them. Such items as a good basic archaeology text, the kind that a university might use as an introduction to an archaeology course, seem logical, as do any reference-type books covering such diverse subjects as bottles, tableware, nails and fasteners, utensils, tools, and other household items. These resources will be helpful for interpreting the various kinds of artifacts that are likely to be found by the young archaeologists. This part of the resource base will grow in the direction and rate dictated by the sites chosen and the intellectual needs of the teacher involved.

A big part of the growing resource collection will be in the form of workbooks, activity kits, simulation games, and computer software. These are items that will help to nurture and maintain the interest level of the students. In time, teachers will likely add their own self-designed and trial-tested materials to the collection.

A listing of available resources, by type, can be found as Appendix A in the back of this book.

Seeking Professional Advice

While literature in various forms is helpful, even necessary, to the successful initiation of your project, of equal importance is getting the advice of a real professional. This is not as difficult as it might seem. Most schools are but a short distance from a college or university, and most of these institutions have an anthropology department with archaeologists more than willing to spread the gospel of correct procedures to interested teachers. Archaeologists realize that successful communication to, and clear understanding by, the public of such important matters as site protection and preservation calls for an enlightened laity; and there is no better way of accomplishing this than by first reaching our elementary and secondary school teachers who in turn have direct—and influential—contact with the next generation of potential site stewards. Networking through well-informed teachers will be seen as a great opportunity by most archaeologists.

Forming an alliance with a professional archaeologist can have numerous side benefits. In addition to answering specific questions about your site, he or she could provide you with helpful literature for your library and may even be receptive to an invitation to come to your school and talk to your young diggers in person.

☞ Activity #1 ☞

Remember that you bring something to the relationship between you and an archaeologist of equal—or even greater—value than the archaeologist's expertise. We are, of course, referring to your own pedagogical skills and professionalism as a teacher and motivator of young students. It is your job to take the professional advice given by the archaeologist and apply it in a manner that you surely know best.

And who knows, the archaeologist might well receive a valuable lesson in pedagogics from you.

> Ironclad Rule #2—You, not the archaeologist, are the expert at teaching children, so make the archaeological material fit your needs.

Tools Needed

Unlike carpenters, mechanics, or even medical doctors, archaeologists do not have their own occupation-specific tool kits. Their tools have been borrowed from the various jobs for which they were originally designed and put to successful adaptive reuse. How often we see the stereotypical archaeologist represented by a pith-helmet-wearing and khaki-shorted individual proudly brandishing the symbolic tools of office, the trowel (thanks to the mason), and the whisk broom (ditto to the housekeeper).

Fortunately, most of the tools necessary to run a successful dig and post-excavation archaeology laboratory are easily attainable and relatively inexpensive. Those items that cost a little more initially—like the shovels and spades—will last for years with proper care, making even their purchase cost-effective. Every moderately well-equipped archaeology project will include the following items:

Large Tools

pick or mattock   wheelbarrow (if called for)
polyethylene sheets (8' x 100" roll)
shovels (both long- and short-handled and square- and round-ended)

Small Tools

trowels (mason's)	whisk brooms
3-meter tapes	30-meter tape
mason's twine	hammer (heavy—for pounding stakes)
awls	paintbrushes
dental picks	dustpans
compass (good quality surveyor's model)	colanders
atomizers or small bellows	buckets
pruning shears	lopping shears
files (mill bastards)	magnifying glasses
gloves	

Specially Built Equipment

table screen	hand screens
wooden stakes (1" x 1" x 15")	

Some of the tools will be initially more expensive than others—the shovels, 30-meter tape, wheelbarrow (if you need one), lopping shears, pick or mattock, and so forth—but they will last for years, given proper care. They amount to a one-time investment. Still other tools may not always be called for but are nice to have on hand.

Some teachers (maybe most?) want to get right into it. And although they would like to accumulate at least a fair inventory of the tools listed above, the immediate need is for something on the order of a "starter kit." To this end I offer the following suggestions: A minimal tool kit (one, let's say, that a university would require for a first-dig course) should include: a mason's trowel (5"), an awl or ice pick, a 3-meter retractable tape, paintbrushes, marking pen, whisk broom, scissors, ball of twine, a compass, and a pair of gloves. Finally, a tackle box or similar container makes a nice tool kit.

> A teacher can put together a basic tool kit in one of two ways: He or she can accumulate a set of tools—all of which are readily available at a local hardware store—and direct the class to put together a similar kit for themselves. The second approach, which some may find more pedagogically appealing, is to make an activity out of the process.

☞ Activities #2 & #3 ☞

Although the teacher should retain a "model" kit for the youngsters to appreciate, students can be encouraged to make substitutions with items commonly found in the average home. For instance, a knitting needle could be used in lieu of an awl or ice pick, or a gardening trowel (it's curved) might be used instead of the less familiar—and flat—mason's trowel. Sometimes students will bring in tools that work better than those in common use. Don't discourage such moves; rather, take the attitude that if it works, fine. As time goes along, each person naturally modifies their tool collection to match particular needs.

Tools are tools, not toys. Youngsters must be made aware of this. Many of the tools, brandished carelessly, can do great physical harm. Teachers must be conscious of the potential dangers and know which tools are safe in the hands of youngsters and which should only be wielded by adults. In the younger grades, for instance, it might be better to exclude the awl or ice pick from the kit.

Archaeologists, like other craftspeople, must take proper care of their tools. Shovels and trowels, used in damp soil and not properly cleaned, dried, and lightly rubbed with an oil-soaked rag, will soon develop a thick patina of rust, which is not only ugly and unprofessional looking but also inhibitive of the tools' most efficient use.

Forms and Work Sheets

Forms are an integral part of archaeological fieldwork. A distinction can be made between *forms*, which are used by archaeologists to record their site data in an efficient and accurate manner, and *work sheets*, which may not be directly related to the data being recovered during the dig but are exercises for honing the skills involved in the recovery process. There are many kinds of basic archaeological forms, and all archae-

ologists have their own pet forms, ones that fit their needs best. The same will be true for the elementary or secondary school teacher. Sample work sheets can be found at the end of each chapter, along with lesson plans and related activities.

Not all forms will be relevant to your excavation. You won't need burial or petroglyph forms, for instance. On the other hand, you may well find a need to devise a form especially for the particular site you've chosen to dig. You can make devising forms a part of your curriculum and allow students to participate in their creation. The forms included herein (see "Maintaining Field Records") are but a suggested sampling of the total available. Use them as they stand, or modify them to fit your needs. All of them are easily duplicated on most word processing programs.

Appendix B is a series of useful and time-tested forms that can be photocopied, modified, or both.

What Makes a Good Site

The definition of a "good" site depends on one's goals. If an anthropologist is looking for specific data to help answer some vexatious archaeological question, then the "good" site is one that provides such data. What defines a "good" site for the elementary or secondary school teacher is its accessibility and its potential as an instructional tool.

Accessibility has to do with how easy it is to transport the students and tools to and from the site. The ideal location for an experimental site would be immediately contiguous to the school; and, of course, in many cases, especially in rural or suburban settings, such a fortuity is possible. Obviously, however, not everyone will find themselves conveniently situated adjacent to an empty lot, and travel distance may ultimately determine the feasibility of the project.

As an instructional tool, the site should contain all the elements necessary to demonstrate the spectrum of skills and concepts utilized by archaeologists. An ideal site will have discernible stratigraphic levels; a wide range of artifacts and artifact types; subterranean features like foundations, floors, pilings, pits, and so forth; faunal remains; recognizable soil changes; and so forth. A site is "user friendly" when its very appearance evokes a positive response in the people called upon to dig it. Surface indications of what might lie below, such as a stone wall or section of floor, will function to hold the youngsters' interest. They serve as constant reminders to the hardworking excavators that there really is something under all that dirt. Finding "clues to the past" or just "old stuff"—and to children anything older than themselves is ancient history—is the carrot that drives the enthusiasm along at full throttle.

Keep a Journal

Archaeologists keep ongoing journals. They usually refer to them as Feature 1 or just F-1 notes (Feature 1 representing the site and the excavation thereof), and they are arguably the most important part of the archaeological project. They tie everything together. A dig is, by its very nature, a complex undertaking, one with a multitude of dimensions and ever-changing complexions. In order to stay on top of everything that is going on and to help ensure that a minimal number of subtle clues are missed, the archaeologist takes voluminous notes. Later on, when report-writing time comes or when he or she sits over a table full of specimens and stone-cold data, the F-1 notes, or journal, becomes a valuable tool in jogging the memory. Your students (and you) can use it the same way, but as a teacher you gain additional profit from it.

Assessment

A daily log kept by your students is an excellent assessment tool. They write down their observations as they go, and periodically (you can decide when) hand them in for review and class discussion. The journals will keep the excavation and laboratory processes "alive" and available to them even after the actual work is long done. Along the way, the journals can help you to keep a check on which aspects of your dig are getting across and which aren't. At the project's end, each student will have a record of what they learned and accomplished, and you, the teacher, will have a capstone assessment instrument.

☞ Activity #4 ☞

TAKING CARE OF ESSENTIALS:
ACTIVITIES AND WORK SHEETS

ACTIVITY NO. 1

Activity:	Who Do You Call?
Subjects:	Language Arts, Science, Social Studies
Rationale:	This activity provides an opportunity for students to (1) learn which experts and professionals are employed to handle various archaeological jobs; and (2) compile an actual resource list of local experts who can be called upon for help as the archaeological project progresses.
Objective:	The students will (1) discuss the various jobs that are involved in work on an archaeological site; (2) make a list of the individuals who could be called upon to provide expertise in various areas; (3) compile a real directory of local resource people who can be utilized at various stages in the archaeological project; and (4) write a letter to a local archaeologist to inform him or her of plans to excavate and ask for advice.
Activity Preparation:	Discuss an archaeological dig and all of the tasks involved from beginning to end.

Activity:

☞ Have students make a list of the many different aspects of a dig about which an expert might be called upon to offer help or advice.

☞ Make an archaeological directory of the addresses and phone numbers of local resource people.

☞ Write a class letter to a local archaeologist about your planned dig. Ask his or her advice.

Materials Needed:

pens or pencils   paper
telephone directory   list of professional archaeologists*
bulletins from local universities**

    *See Appendix A—*Archaeologists of the Americas*
    **These are readily available from local colleges and universities
      in care of the Admissions Office

Vocabulary:

archaeologist
anthropologist
expertise
site

ACTIVITY NO. 2

Activity:	Building an Archaeology Kit
Subjects:	Motor Skills, Science
Rationale:	This activity provides an opportunity for students to (1) learn what daily activities are required of a field archaeologist; and (2) what tools are commonly utilized in their work.
Objectives:	The students will (1) discuss the various jobs that are a part of the daily field routine; (2) compile a list of tools and discuss their proper use; (3) make a list of common household items that could be used in an archaeologist's kit; and (4) collect as many of the necessary small tools as they can.

Activity Preparation:

☞ Discuss the routine duties of the field archaeologist.

☞ Show the students the tools from the teacher's model kit and discuss their names, proper use, and care.

Activity:

☞ Make a list of common household items that might be substituted for, or supplement, those in the teacher's kit.

☞ Have the students bring to school, in a proper container, their individual "starter" kits.

Materials Needed:

trowel
whisk broom
3-meter tape
twine
awl or ice pick (adjust to grade level)
paintbrushes
compass
scissors
marking pen
gloves
tackle box (or similar container)

ACTIVITY NO. 3

Activity:	Making an Excavator's Scoop
Subjects:	Art, Science
Rationale:	This manual activity will offer the students the opportunity to construct a useful archaeological tool.
Objectives:	Students will each make an excavator's scoop that can be used in their archaeological fieldwork.

Activity Preparation:

☞ Show the class a scoop made from a large plastic bleach (or similar) bottle. Explain its use as a tool.

☞ Using a whole bleach bottle and a thick felt marking pen, outline on the container the area to be cut out to form the scoop.

☞ Using scissors, cut along the black lines creating a scoop.

Activity:

☞ Have each student bring a large, empty bleach bottle or similar container to class.

☞ Hand out black markers and direction sheets.

☞ Have the students mark their bottles accordingly.

☞ *Carefully* handling the scissors, have the students cut out their scoops (teachers must decide whether or not their students are mature enough to do the cutting themselves).

☞ Using colored markers, have the young archaeologists individualize or decorate their newly made scoops.

Materials Needed:

large bleach bottles
thick black felt markers
colored permanent markers
scissors
direction sheets

Making an Archaeological Scoop

1) Get a large, plastic bleach bottle (Make sure you leave the cap on!)

2) Using a black felt marker, put lines where shown

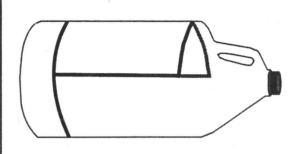

3) Using scissors, carefully cut along the black lines to form your scoop

4) Decorate your finished product in your own personal style!

ACTIVITY NO. 4

Activity:	Keeping a Journal
Subjects:	Language Arts, Science, Social Studies
Rationale:	This activity will (1) help to make students more observant; and (2) serve as a means for assessing what they have learned.
Objectives:	Students will each maintain a daily journal of the archaeological project.

Activity Preparation:

☞ Discuss with the class the relative complexity of the project. Explain how the keeping of a *journal,* or *log,* helps to keep things fresh in the mind and can also be referred to at a later time.

☞ Explain how journals are personal *observations* and that each individual may look at things in slightly different ways. Journals may have drawings or sketches as well as prose. They may also contain photographs.

Activity:

☞ Direct students to bring a notebook to class that will be used as their daily journal of the dig.

☞ Allow students time during the project period to take notes on what is going on around them.

☞ At the end of each phase of the archaeological unit, have the students read selections from their journals as to what they have noted.

☞ Discuss the observations.

Materials Needed:
notebooks
pens or pencils

Vocabulary:
journal
log
observations

DISCUSSING EXPECTATIONS

Terms and Concepts

Like the coach with his "skull session" preceding the big football game, the teacher should spend some time discussing what might be expected once the crew is in the field. This is not so much a discussion of the physical aspects of the site—although, of course, that may be part of it—as it is an examination of what kind of things might be found and what they might mean. In a sense it is defining what archaeology is and what its potentials, limitations, and so forth are. Pre-field classroom experiments can help to frame some of these concepts.

Try "excavating" a student's desk, or perhaps better, the teacher's wastepaper basket. Show how careful attention to the position and layering (stratigraphy, to the archaeologist) of the various items in the basket can be interpreted to tell us things about the people who filled it. Let the imaginations soar! Caution the wildly extravagant, but, as in brainstorming sessions, do not discourage Icarian flights. You never know from where a great idea may come.

Start by making a list of the terms and concepts that you will want to incorporate into your lesson. The glossary of terms included at the end of this section is in no way intended to be exhaustive, but more a good starting point. This glossary of words should not only be verbalized, but demonstrated. *Artifacts,* for example, are the basic unit of study in archaeology. They are to the archaeologist what elements are to the chemist. You can define the term in words that the youngsters will understand, *but,* you will want to reinforce this definition by allowing them to see and handle real artifacts. First, show them some prehistoric artifacts such as projectile points, stone axes, clamshell beads, pottery shards—whatever you have available—and discuss their probable uses and functions. Encourage specific discussion about the objects. See how many descriptive characteristics students can come up with. Discuss how form relates to function. Persuade them to look at objects in new ways and to see things from other perspectives. A large part of archaeological interpretation entails this very process. After a bit, introduce some artifacts representative of a historical era—some old utensils, machine parts, tools, and so forth, should serve nicely in this capacity. Continue with the same kind of artifact-specific discussion. Finally, bring forward your thoroughly modern artifacts—chalk, pencils, notebooks—and discuss how much of what you are looking at now will survive the rigors of time and the environment and be preserved for future study. Show how these items may be commonplace to us, but, like the projectile points and old tools before them, will someday be the subject matter of an archaeologist's puzzle. In short, get them accustomed to seeing the totality of the artifact.

☞ Activities #5, #6, #7, & #8 ☜

Once the vocabulary is taken care of you can pass on to some of the more complex issues such as: What are the uses of archaeology? How do sites differ from one another? What limitations are there? What effect does time have on sites? Or environment? What is site vandalism? How does vandalism affect the archaeological record? The issues introduced here can be a part of the class discussion, to one extent or another, throughout the rest of the program. They are questions that are always pertinent, and ones which, as the children's experience grows, you can return to with deeper understanding.

Along with the instillment which naturally follows on the heels of repeated discussion of the terms and concepts, an imaginative teacher can, by proper orchestration and example, ensure that the youngsters are primed and ready to get their hands dirty in their first organized excavation.

DISCUSSING EXPECTATIONS:
ACTIVITIES, WORK SHEETS, AND GLOSSARY

ACTIVITY NO. 5

Activity: Site in a Bag

Subjects: Social Studies, Science, Language Arts

Rationale: This activity will (1) help students to understand the role of context in archaeological interpretation; (2) help to hone their analytical and interpretative skills; and (3) demonstrate how archaeologists can draw conclusions about people from their artifacts.

Objectives: The students will (1) select several personal artifacts from home that tell something about themselves; and (2) will examine and analyze the artifacts brought in by others to determine as much as they can about the owners.

Activity Preparation:

☞ Discuss the concept of *context.* Show with examples how we can often determine the use or function of an unfamiliar object by seeing it in close *association* with an object or other item with which we are familiar. First show the unfamiliar artifact; discuss its shape and other *attributes.* Point out how some attributes give clues to possible uses. Second, show an item with which the students are familiar. Finally, put the two together in their natural context to show how it helps us to determine function or use.

☞ Show how a group of artifacts is more informative than a single one when it comes to telling us something about the user. For example, hold up a ballpoint pen and ask what it tells us about the user. After discussing the limitations, add a gender- or age-associated artifact to show how it increases our knowledge. Discuss how archaeologists can learn much more about a site's inhabitants from artifacts in context, or association, than without context.

Activity:

☞ Give students bags and ask them to each put in five or six objects (artifacts) that tell something about themselves. Nothing with names or other identifying marks should be used.

☞ "Code" the bags for identification and then pass them out—making sure no one gets his or her own.

☞ One at a time, have students show the artifacts in their respective bags and have the others draw conclusions about the artifacts, short of guessing whose they are.

26

ACTIVITY NO. 5

☞ When all of the artifacts have been displayed, have the class guess the owners.

☞ Discuss the activity. Why were some bags easier to identify than others? Did having more than one artifact help? Why? How does the exercise relate to archaeology?

Materials Needed:　bags
marking pen (for coding bags)
various personal artifacts

Vocabulary:　context
association
artifacts
attributes

ACTIVITY NO. 6

Activity:	What in the World?
Subjects:	Social Studies, Science, Language Arts
Rationale:	This activity helps students (1) to recognize artifacts as to function and use; (2) to identify *salient,* or key artifactual, *attributes* that help to identify them; and (3) to appreciate the difficulty of identifying some artifacts when they are found out of context.
Objectives:	Students will (1) find an unusual artifact at home (historic or prehistoric) whose use is not obvious; (2) the class will make a list of what they think are salient attributes for each artifact; and (3) the class will then discuss to what other uses the artifacts might have been put.
Activity Preparation:	Discuss *artifact attributes.* Show the class some common and less common artifacts and point out what are called *salient attributes*—physical attributes that are important clues to the function of the artifact.

Activity:

☞ Have students bring an unusual artifact from home. It may be prehistoric or historic. [**Note:** Teacher should have some artifacts on hand in case some fail to comply.]

☞ Working in small groups, have the students identify the artifacts and their likely use.

☞ Have each group make a list of attributes which would have made the artifact easier to interpret.

☞ Discuss how the in-site context would help make the artifact less ambiguous.

Materials Needed: Objects brought by students
Some unusual artifacts

Vocabulary: artifact
attribute
in situ
function
context
salient attribute

ACTIVITY NO. 7

Activity: Shape and Material Equals Function

Subjects: Science, Social Studies, Language Arts, Art

Rationale: This activity provides the opportunity for students to understand (1) how the function of a tool can be determined by its shape and material; and (2) the differences between primary and secondary, and simple and complex tools.

Objectives: The students will demonstrate an awareness of the relationship between an artifact's shape and material and its ultimate use.

Activity Preparation:

☞ Discuss how prehistoric peoples made their tools out of available *material.* Show several examples of how different materials like stone, bone, shell, or wood have different qualities that make them suitable for different uses.

☞ Using pictures, real artifacts (tools or utensils), or both, explain the difference between *primary* (tools that serve an end directly, such as a knife) and *secondary tools* (tools used to make other tools such as a whetstone) and between *simple* (consisting of only one part) and *complex tools* (those made up of more than one part).

Activity:

☞ Distribute pictures of prehistoric artifacts among the students and have the students draw the artifacts as close to scale as they can.

☞ The students will decide, based on the material and shape, the artifacts' use.

☞ From the tools and utensils available, each student selects and draws (again, to scale) a modern artifact used in the same way.

☞ Discuss the issues involved.

Materials Needed: photographs of various prehistoric artifacts
tools and utensils
drawing paper (with gridlines) or graph paper
pens and pencils

Vocabulary: material
primary tools
simple tools
secondary tools
complex tools

ACTIVITY NO. 8

Activity:	Wastebasket Archaeology
Subjects:	Science, Social Studies, Language Arts
Rationale:	This exercise will show students (1) how stratigraphy, or the layering of materials, helps to date the objects relative to one another; and (2) how the association of artifacts in a confined area offers clues to the activity taking place there.
Objectives:	Students will (1) demonstrate their understanding of *stratigraphy,* and (2) be able to categorize the found materials by their use or function.

Activity Preparation:

☞ Collect wastebaskets from several predetermined locations. [**Note:** Select baskets from rooms or areas that show distinct, demonstrable differences, e.g., cafeteria, library, principal's office, different grade levels.]

☞ Using the wastebasket from your own classroom as a "site," explain how sites are formed. Ask the students to discuss the meaning of the waste and what it tells us. What items went into it first? What last? Discuss *stratigraphy* and the *law of superposition.* Discuss *relative dating,* that is, the dating of something relative to something else rather than a measure of time. Example: "Older than" or "younger than" as opposed to "six weeks old" or "4,000 B.C. ," and so forth. What do the waste materials tell us about the room from which the basket came?

☞ Using chalk, circle the wastebasket with lines separating it into three *layers,* or levels. From the top, mark them 1, 2, 3.

☞ Carefully go through the basket removing each piece of material one at a time. Place the material into three discrete piles representing the different layers (or *strata*) in the basket.

Activity:

☞ Divide the students into groups and have each group choose a different wastebasket.

☞ After dividing the basket into three layers, carefully "excavate" each basket separating the recovered materials by layer. Carefully record the contents using the accompanying Activity Work Sheet.

☞ Categorize the recovered materials by their function or use.

ACTIVITY NO. 8

Groups decide the original location (*provenience* to the archaeologist) of their wastebasket based on its contents.

Materials Needed: wastebaskets from various school locations
Activity Work Sheets
Stratigraphic Data Record sheets
pencils
chalk

Vocabulary: stratigraphy
context
law of superposition
layer
stratum
provenience
relative dating
midden

31

WASTEBASKET ARCHAEOLOGY WORK SHEET

Cafeteria

People throw things away that they no longer need or want. Collections of such discarded material, which we call dumps, or landfills, are known by the archaeologist as *middens*. They are packed full of valuable information. Why?

In today's world we commonly put our trash or discards into trash cans or wastebaskets. We can compare the modern trash container to the ancient midden and "dig" it in the same careful manner as the archaeologist excavates his or her midden.

Let the wastebasket be your midden. Separate it into three layers (or strata), and carefully remove the contents one piece at a time. Separate the contents by strata, using the Stratigraphic Data Sheet to record the contents.

☞ Which layer (or stratum) has the oldest (or earliest deposited) material? Which the newest? How can you tell?

☞ What do our observations tell us about the creation of real archaeological sites?

☞ Being careful to keep the strata separate, divide the material in each stratum by its apparent function or use. What apparent activities can be identified with each stratum?
- •
- •
- •
- •

☞ What can you tell about the people who used this wastebasket?

☞ What room do you think it came from? How did you reach this conclusion?

STRATIGRAPHIC DATA SHEET

Layer (Stratum) One

1.	11.	21.
2.	12.	22.
3.	13.	23.
4.	14.	24.
5.	15.	25.
6.	16.	26.
7.	17.	27.
8.	18.	28.
9.	19.	29.
10.	20.	30.

Layer (Stratum) Two

1.	11.	21.
2.	12.	22.
3.	13.	23.
4.	14.	24.
5.	15.	25.
6.	16.	26.
7.	17.	27.
8.	18.	28.
9.	19.	29.
10.	20.	30.

Layer (Stratum) Three

1.	11.	21.
2.	12.	22.
3.	13.	23.
4.	14.	24.
5.	15.	25.
6.	16.	26.
7.	17.	27.
8.	18.	28.
9.	19.	29.
10.	20.	30.

GLOSSARY

Absolute Dating: A dating method that assigns dates or ages in calendar years or which references a fixed date. *Absolute dating* is often referred to as *chronometric dating*.

Examples: "5000 B.C.," "1776," "40 years ago," "1997," and "8 years old" are all examples of absolute dates. "Older than," "younger than," and "same age as" are examples of *relative dates*.

Activity Area: A place on a site where a *specific* activity took place, usually determined by the kind of *artifacts* and *features* found there.

Examples: The *activity areas* of your house, for example, would be the kitchen, bathroom, living room, dining room, and so forth.

Artifact: Anything made, modified, or altered by human use.

Examples: Arrowheads, knives, pens, paper, bracelets, baseballs, clothing, ornaments—in short, *everything!* [**Note:** While a building or other structure is also an artifact—because it is made by humans—it is so large, immovable, and consists of many smaller artifacts (each brick and cut stone is an artifact) which archaeologists would refer to as *features*.]

Archaeology: The study of the human past through material remains. The principal aims are to determine what happened, to whom it happened, when it happened, and finally, why it happened.

Example: Like a detective arriving at the scene of the crime and using clues to find out who did what to whom and why, *archaeologists* use recovered artifacts and other data to piece together the past. Call them "detectives of the past."

Association: The close physical relationship between two or more pieces of archaeological data.

Example: The charcoal and bones contained in an Indian fire pit are said to be in *association*. We can learn much more when artifacts are in association than when they are found alone because we can see the actual way in which they were used. If you didn't know what a hammer was for, finding it next to a nail—which you did recognize—would tell you about the hammer.

Context: The relationship of material remains in time and space; the arrangement or setting in which things are found.

Examples: Artifacts, arranged as they are found by the archaeologist, are said to

be in *context*. Artifacts arranged in a museum display are not in context.

Contract Archaeology: Archaeology carried out under a special contract or agreement with a public or private agency or company.

Examples: An engineering firm that is building a dam will make an agreement with archaeologists to have the area where the dam is being constructed investigated to assure that no archaeological sites will be destroyed by the dam-building or the lake that forms behind it.

Cultural Resource: Remains that make up our nonrenewable (irreplaceable) heritage from the past.

Examples: Oil, gas, coal, timber, and minerals are called natural resources. Prehistoric sites, buildings, historic sites, battlefields, and so forth, are *cultural resources*.

Ecofacts: Nonartifactual material—like charcoal, seeds, bones, and so forth—from a site that, though not human-made, nevertheless has cultural relevance.

Examples: *Ecofacts,* while not in themselves artifacts (they haven't been made or altered for use), nevertheless owe their presence in the site to the humans there. If a person were to eat a chicken leg and toss aside the bone, the bone would be considered an *ecofact.* If someone were to make a whistle of it, it would be considered an artifact.

Excavation: The careful recovery of buried objects (artifacts and ecofacts) in relation to their level and other associated objects with which they occur.

Examples: Digging is just creating a hole by the removal of dirt. *Excavation* includes the extremely careful attention to detail, much more than simply moving dirt.

Feature: A name that archaeologists give to any nonmovable archaeological remains that indicate human activity but cannot be removed without destroying the remains' integrity.

Examples: Although technically *artifacts,* some remains cannot be moved without destroying them. Specific examples would include fire pits, floors, walls, wells, all buildings, and so forth.

Grid, or Site Grid: The pattern of small squares into which a site is divided prior to excavation and that is used to note the precise horizontal location of things found in the site.

Examples: The squares, usually separated from each other by stakes and strings, allow the archaeologist to pinpoint from where everything recovered comes.

Historical Archaeology: That subfield of archaeology concerned with the time period in which the societies being studied had written records of their activities.

Examples: *Historical archaeology* concerns sites that existed when writing had become available.

Industry: All of the artifacts made from the same material that come from the same site.

Examples: Things made from bone are the bone *industry,* things from stone, the stone, or lithic (Latin for stone), *industry,* and so on. Modern artifacts are far more complex because there are so many more kinds of material now than in prehistoric times.

In Situ: The Latin term meaning "in its original place," used in reference to things in an archaeological site that have not been moved from their original location.

Examples: An artifact found in the ground is *in situ.* An artifact found by screening the dirt is not *in situ.*

Law of Superposition: The principle that objects or material buried or deposited earliest will be found deepest in the ground and those buried later will be found higher up. The *law of superposition* is a means of dating things by the layer, or *stratum,* that they are in.

Examples: Look in your clothes hamper. The dirty socks you threw in last week are on the bottom; the shirt or blouse with yesterday's pizza glob is on top.

Layer, or Level: A horizontal volume of earth that is distinct from that which lies above it and below it. Items in the same layer are thought to have come from roughly the same time period.

Examples: A person chooses a plot of land on which to build a house (one layer). The house burns down, leaving a pile of ashes and debris (another layer). A flooding river covers the house remains with three feet of mud (another layer). Someone comes along and builds a

parking lot on top of it all (still another layer). These make up *layers*.

Lithics: Artifacts made from stone.

Examples: Arrowheads, spear points, tomahawks, tombstones, statues, pillars, and so forth are examples of *lithics*.

Posthole: A small pit, or hole, that once held a post for the support of a roof. Usually they are a different color than the surrounding soil.

Examples: A wooden pole, or post, that held up a roof has long since decayed, and in its place is a small, darkly stained circle, which is decomposed wood mixed with earth.

Prehistory: That subfield of archaeology concerned with societies that existed before the use of writing or the written record.

Example: It's the opposite, so to speak, of historical archaeology.

Provenience: The specific location of archaeological data within a site.

Examples: When an archaeologist first finds an artifact in the site, its position is carefully noted for later reference. The artifact's *provenience* is precisely where it came from in the site.

Relative Dating: A method by which dates are assigned without reference to a fixed time scale.

Examples: Relative dates are *not* in years as are absolute dates. Instead, terms such as "younger than," "older than," and "same age as" are used in *relative dating*. *Stratigraphy* is a good example of a relative dating technique.

Site: Any place, large or small, that shows evidence of previous human activity or occupation.

Examples: Sites can be as small as an overnight camping spot or as large as a village or town. All places where human activities occur are potential *sites*.

Site Number: A distinct number given to each archaeological site.

Examples: *Site numbers* allow archaeologists to keep track of sites. Most U.S. site numbers consist of three sets of numbers and letters. For instance, in site 33 MH 9, the "33" stands for Ohio (the 33rd state alphabetically), the "MH" stands for Mahoning County (the Ohio county in which the site is located), and "9" refers to the ninth site recorded in that county.

Salvage Archaeology: Archaeology done on an emergency basis because a site is in imminent danger of being destroyed.

Examples: Sometimes archaeologists are called in because a highway construction crew has stumbled on an archaeological site. In such a case, as with a medical emergency, the work must be done quickly and often with less thought than one would like.

Stratigraphy: The study of geological or archaeological layering at a site; that is, the analysis of the *strata.*

Examples: Site layers sitting one atop the other show relationships and how one layer relates to another. You try to read the soil layers like someone else would read a book.

Stratum: A horizontal level, or layer, in a site. The plural is *strata.*

Examples: *Stratum* means the same thing as layer, or level.

Survey: The close examination of an area prior to land alteration activities in order to see if there are any sites present that might be damaged or destroyed.

Examples: Agencies and companies sometimes have an archaeologist do a walkover *survey* of an area on which they plan to build, mine, or alter in some way.

Test Pit: A pit or hole dug to determine site depth, stratigraphic sequences, and so forth, prior to excavation.

Examples: *Test pits* are dug to determine the presence of sites. They are also used to determine what the layering looks like. It's the archaeologist's way of "peeking" underground.

Unit: Specifically designated squares within a site which allow the archaeologist to keep control of where archaeological materials are found and what they are associated with.

Examples: By carefully assigning each *unit* with a different designation, the archaeologist can keep close track of the location, or *provenience,* of the remains.

THE WORKING HYPOTHESES

Scientific Methodology

One of the major goals of a course like this one is to teach youngsters the gist of what constitutes the "scientific method," an understanding of which they will find useful in almost anything they do. It is ironic that while most individuals can tell "science" from "non-science"—or at least they think they can—few (including many teachers of science) can adequately describe the scientific method.

Regardless of the type of study undertaken, all scientific research—and archaeology is scientific research—must proceed through several well-defined steps. These steps are: (1) formulation of a hypothesis (or even better, hypotheses); (2) explanation of the procedures to be employed (this is the research design that states explicitly how what you are going to do in the field is going to prove or disprove your hypotheses); (3) acquisition of the data (these are your actual field excavation and recovered data); (4) analysis of the data (what is done with the archaeological data once they are back in the lab or classroom and ready for examination); and (5) verification (seeing whether or not the data support the hypotheses).

✑ Activities #9 & #10 ✑

The *hypothesis* is the basic foundation upon which the scientific methodology is built. Scientific knowledge cannot grow without it as it serves as a bridge between speculation, or "guessing," and verification. A useful hypothesis is one that is conceptually clear and unambiguous ("All crows are black"); related to objective and readily observable phenomena ("Ice melts at a lower temperature than glass"); specific and simple; testable (students ought to be able to devise a test that would prove or disprove the accuracy of their hypotheses); plausible (it should meet the test of logical possibility); and meaningful (it should be worth knowing). Examples of all kinds can be used to demonstrate these concepts. Spend some time developing hypotheses that fit the above criteria about various things within the classroom. Once you've done that, run them through the remaining three methodological steps and discuss the outcomes. Which ones met the rigorous standards demanded of the scientific method? Which didn't? Why?

Establishing Your Hypotheses

Now you are ready to have the class put its newly acquired methodological skills to work on the actual archaeological work at hand. Using what foreknowledge of the site you have, set about devising your "working" hypotheses with the class. *A working*

hypothesis is one which is framed prior to doing the fieldwork and, to a great extent, determines the manner and means by which the dig is carried out. The working hypothesis tells us what specific kinds of observations to make and what data to collect. An example: If our hypothesis is that individual room use in our excavated structure will be reflected in the type of artifacts found within each, then we must design a method of observing and collecting the field data that will allow us to accurately verify (or not) this hypothesis. For instance, we would be required to excavate and discretely collect by room rather than by an arbitrarily established grid system that in all likelihood would merge material from different rooms.

Notice we said working hypotheses—the emphasis being definitely on the plural. Before undertaking fieldwork and data collection, it is preferable to have several hypotheses available for testing simultaneously. In the event that one or another does not pan out, you can concentrate on the others.

Some Suggested Site Hypotheses

The following list is not in any way intended to be exhaustive but only to serve as a starting point for your excavations. Each individual site is expected to yield a different set of questions which need testing.

Hypothesis: The type, range, and frequency of artifacts at a site will be an indication of the activity that was carried out there.

Hypothesis: The specific location of various artifacts and remains within a site will reflect areas where specific activities took place.

Hypothesis: As some artifacts tend to be gender-related, the absence, presence, and frequencies of such will provide clues to the sexual breakdown of the occupying population.

Hypothesis: As some artifacts tend to be age-related, the absence, presence, and frequencies of such will provide clues to the age breakdown of the occupying population.

Hypothesis: The thickness of the site deposit is an indication of how long the site was occupied.

Hypothesis: The date of the artifacts found is an indication of the date of the site's use.

Hypothesis: Commercial sites will contain a minimal number of household artifacts.

As you can see, the list is limited only by the imagination of the group. Some hypotheses are more general than others and can easily be split into a multitude of specific subhypotheses for even closer examination. For example, instead of testing the broader hypothesis, to wit, "The specific location of various types of artifacts in a site will reflect the activities carried out there," we could say, more specifically, "The finding of an abundance of artifacts associated with food preparation and faunal remains (butchered bones) in one area of the site indicates that it was, in all likelihood, the kitchen." *You can get as specific as you want—as long as it's testable.* The examples above are, for the most part, verifiable in the archaeological record, but even those not likely to be so are still valuable for teaching youngsters the scientific method.

Ironclad Rule #3—Don't dismiss student-initiated hypotheses out of hand. Even those you feel will not test out, or on the surface appear to be untrue, should be examined. Remember, this is a learning experience, and just as much can be learned from an unsound hypothesis as a sound one.

THE WORKING HYPOTHESES:
ACTIVITIES AND WORK SHEETS

ACTIVITY NO. 9

Activity: What Do You See?

Subjects: Science, Language Arts

Rationale: This exercise will help students to (1) hone their observational skills; and (2) form *conclusions* based on their observations.

Objectives: The students will demonstrate their abilities to examine things with a critical attention to detail and to draw sound *conclusions* from their observations.

Activity Preparation:

☞ Explain to the students how the observable qualities and *attributes* of things are a reflection of other, less obvious, information. Point out how careful *observation* of details can allow us to draw *conclusions* about other things not so readily apparent.

☞ Bring an unusual object (tool or utensil) from home and ask the class to make a list of *observations* about it. Write them on the board.

☞ Have the students list which observations have a direct bearing on the object's use and which do not. Discuss.

Activity:

☞ Form the class into small groups and give each group an object (try to make it as unusual as you can).

☞ Using the accompanying work sheet, have each student list as many observations as he or she can about the object.

☞ Have each student list *conclusions* drawn from his or her observations.

☞ Compare results and discuss.

Materials Needed: several unusual objects from home
Activity Work Sheets
pens or pencils

Vocabulary: observation
attributes
conclusions

OBSERVATION WORK SHEET

Observations

Conclusions based on observations

What could you do to verify your conclusions?

ACTIVITY NO. 10

Activity:	Forming and Testing Hypotheses
Subjects:	Science, Language Arts
Rationale:	This activity will improve the ability of students to (1) frame simple hypothetical statements; and (2) devise tests to verify (prove or disprove) these *hypotheses*.
Objectives:	The students will demonstrate their abilities to (1) draw *hypotheses* based on *observations;* and (2) devise workable tests to verify or disprove these *hypotheses* or *conclusions*.

Activity Preparation:

☞ Explain to the students how close, direct *observation* allows us to draw *conclusions* about what we are looking at. Discuss the difference between important and less important observations. Explain *verification*. Show how properly devised tests can show which conclusions are likely to be true and which are not.

☞ Show some pictures of various scenes and ask the students to make a list of their *direct* observations. After some discussion, show each picture again and solicit suggestions as to what other things are not directly observable that we can say about the scene. For example: Show a picture of a big house and ask what we might assume (hypothesize) about the people who live there.

☞ Ask the students to supply a list of ways they could verify (prove or disprove) their *hypotheses*. Discuss.

Activity:

☞ Pass out pictures of various scenes.

☞ Have students, using the accompanying work sheet, list as many hypotheses about their pictures or scenes as they can.

☞ For each hypothesis, students will list at least one valid suggestion as to how they could verify (prove or disprove) it.

☞ Compare results and discuss.

Materials Needed:

various pictures from magazines   work sheets
pens or pencils

Vocabulary:

observations   hypotheses
conclusions   verification

HYPOTHESIS FORMATION WORK SHEET

Look closely at the picture that is in front of you. When people look closely at things, they make observations. Some observations are more important than others and can give us less obvious information.

Examine your picture closely.
1. List the *important* observations you can make.

   (1)   (2)

   (3)   (4)

   (5)   (6)

   (7)   (8)

   (9)   (10)

   (11)   (12)

Why are they important?

2. List some less important observations.

   (1)   (2)

   (3)   (4)

   (5)   (6)

Why are they less important?

3. Careful observations often allow us to draw certain conclusions about what we are examining. Based on the observations you listed above as important, what are some conclusions you might draw about the picture?

   (1)   (2)

   (3)   (4)

   (5)   (6)

   (7)   (8)

HYPOTHESIS FORMATION WORK SHEET

4.   The conclusions you draw can be turned into hypotheses ("educated guesses," some might say) which are statements that are *verifiable*. This means they can be tested and proved or disproved. Take this example: Even if you do not directly observe a little girl in the picture, you might note a girl's bike. Therefore, you might conclude, or *hypothesize,* that a little girl lived in the house. What could you do to show whether or not your hypothesis was correct? Take each of your conclusions (*hypotheses*) and list *for each* the way or ways that you could *verify* (prove or disprove) them.

Hypothesis One:

Tests: (a)

(b)

(c)

Hypothesis Two:

Tests: (a)

(b)

(c)

Hypothesis Three:

Tests: (a)

(b)

(c)

Hypothesis Four:

Tests: (a)

(b)

(c)

Hypothesis Five:

Tests: (a)

(b)

(c)

Hypothesis Six:

Tests: (a)

(b)

(c)

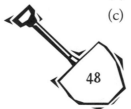

PRE-EXCAVATION RESEARCH

The Site Visit: Observations and Recording

Along with the artifacts and specimens retrieved from a site, archaeologists place considerable importance on the site itself. Geographical, geological, zoological, and botanical aspects of the undug site are important contributors to the determination of the site's ultimate use or function. You can tell a good deal about that empty lot you are about to dig from its surroundings. For instance, a lot surrounded on all sides by standing residences is more likely to have been a residence itself than an industrial site; whereas, one enclosed by a broad, paved parking area is far more likely to have been a commercial site than a domicile.

Forms Versus "Freestyle" Notes

There is a strong case that can be made for using standardized forms to record site information. Forms in common use have evolved to their present state through years of trial and error. Most forms include a minimum of data categories that should be recorded and, as such, are useful as checklists and memory joggers—so long as slavish adherence does not fetter fuller or more imaginative recording. You must not become too reliant on a form to tell you what to record. This is where open-ended note-taking is an advantage.

While forms serve as a constant reminder to the archaeologist of what data are notable, open-ended note-taking relies entirely on the observational skills of the recorder. A notebook, pen or pencil, and a keen perception of what is potentially important is the stuff that allows the archaeologist to go beyond the perimeters of the pre-set form. Which should it be, form or freestyle? Fortunately, it does not have to be entirely one or the other. Why not take a more eclectic approach?

You can devise a form that satisfies the function of providing space for all of the notes and measurements, which obviously must be a part of your permanent record, and, at the same time, contains a large "Comments," "Remarks," or "Observations" section just perfect for the perceptive observer who insists on reaching beyond the confining limits of the standard form.

☞ **Activities #11 & #12** ☜

Appendix B contains a variety of forms. Copy them for use as is or modify them to suit your individual needs.

Teams or Individuals?

One way of carrying out the job of site recording is to break the class up into teams, assigning to each a different set of site-recording jobs. This, of course, has a major advantage in fostering teamwork and cooperative learning. Some, however, may find this advantage offset by the loss of a more well-rounded learning experience and the minimizing of individual creativity and initiative.

One option would be allowing each individual to do his or her own recording and then combining all of the individually collected data, by teamwork, into a single master form. This would add the dimension of allowing students to see the site through the eyes of their fellow "scientists" and would afford them the opportunity to pick up on anything they might have missed.

> **Ironclad Rule #4**—Encourage the youngsters to record copiously, regardless of how unimportant the observations may seem. Such note-taking not only hones students' observational and communicational skills, but also contributes to their knowledge of botany, geology, landscaping, architecture, industry, and so forth.

Maps

Before undertaking site excavation you must provide yourself with at least one copy—preferably more than one—of an official seven-and-a-half-inch quadrangle (that's its size) United States Geological Survey (USGS) topographic map containing your site. These can be purchased locally at engineering supply stores, or at various county offices. A handsome monthly catalog titled New Publications of the U.S. Geological Survey, listing the names, dates, and prices of maps, books, and so forth, and containing order forms, is available free from:

U.S. Geological Survey
582 National Center
Reston, VA 22092

Topographic maps covering any area in the United States are available by addressing your mail orders to:

U.S. Geological Survey, Information Services
Box 25286, Federal Center
Denver, CO 80225

For further map information or assistance in ordering, the U.S. Geological Survey has two toll-free hotlines. Call 1-800-USA-MAPS or 1-800-HELP-MAP. USGS topographic maps from your particular county can usually be purchased at the engi-

neering department in your local county courthouse or you can refer to your local yellow pages for commercial map dealers. Topographic maps of all scales presently sell for $4 each.

Once you have found and marked your site location on a map, it will serve as the source of some of the information you need for accurate recording of your site. A brief lesson in map reading is something that would be helpful in many ways and would fit in nicely here.

☞ Activities #13 & #14 ☞

Determining Your Site's Location on the Map

There are basically two ways of locating sites on the Earth's surface. The older way utilized lines of latitude and longitude to pinpoint location. This system, which proved useful for centuries and is still in wide use by mariners and others, relies on the distance measurements of degrees (°), minutes ('), and seconds ("). The other simpler, but even more accurate, system is called the Universal Transverse Mercator Grid System.

UTM

The past 25 years have seen a shift to the more elegant Universal Transverse Mercator (UTM) Grid System. This system is much easier to work with as it deals entirely in the metric system. In this system, the Earth is broken down into a grid composed of 1,000- by 1,000-meter squares measuring north and south from the equator and east and west from the prime meridian. Not only does the system accurately pinpoint your site location, but it is an excellent mathematical exercise. Once your site is plotted on the USGS map, it is a relatively simple matter to translate its position into locational terms.

Running up the left and right margins of your map and across the upper and lower margins are a series of light blue ticks. These ticks are separated from one another by a linear distance of 1,000 meters. Starting at the lower left-hand corner of the map, these ticks *may* be labeled with a four-digit number consisting of two superscript digits followed by two normal ones; example: 4539. At, or near, the top of the left-hand (or western) margin, this UTM number will appear as a seven-digit number ending in three zeroes in superscript; example: 4552000. The actual number of blue ticks that are numerically labeled depends solely on how "littered" with map data and print the particular map margins are. The right-hand (or eastern) margin has the same number of corresponding ticks, but the labeling system is the reverse, that is, the four-digit label appears at the top of the margin, and the complete seven-digit one appears on the bottom. These numbers refer to the site's *northing*.

UTM Units

Zone

UTM Unit

1000 x 1000 meters

Site

100 x 100 meter

Part of Site

10 x 10 meter

Your Unit

1 x 1 meter

Across the top (northern) or bottom (southern) margin of the map are similar blue 1,000-meter ticks. These ticks are labeled in a west-to-east direction and, unlike the northing numbers, consist of only six digits; example: 532000. This set of numbers gives the site's *easting*.

In the legend at the lower left-hand corner of the map sheet, a zone number is given. This number *must* precede the northing and easting figures.

☞ Activity #15 ☞

Topo Sheet

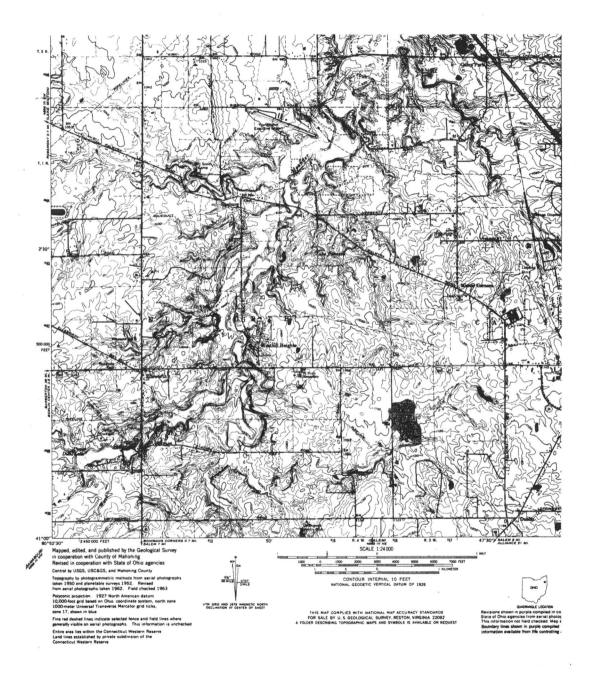

Figuring Your UTM Location

Using a pencil with a very fine point and a professional-quality straightedge, or T-square, connect the corresponding UTM (blue) ticks, from top to bottom margin which are closest to, but *west* of, the site. Be sure that the UTM ticks that you have connected have the same three-digit number. This is your easting reference line. Now connect the UTM ticks, from left to right margin, that are closest to, but *south* of the site. This is your northing reference line. These lines will intersect to the *southwest* of the site.

Copy the portions of the *easting* (three digits) and *northing* (four digits) coordinates given on the quadrangle map. Locate the scale on the coordinate counter that matches that of the quadrangle map (usually 1:4,000) and align the counter so that the horizontal scale, which is read from right to left, is placed along the east-west, or *northing,* reference line. The vertical scale should be aligned to pass directly through the center of the site being located. Read the scales: right to left for the easting and upward for the northing. Round these values (three digits for each) to the nearest 10 meters and enter them on the ends of the three-digit easting and four-digit northing that you have copied down. The completed UTM reference will read: ZONE (two digits), EASTING (six digits), and NORTHING (seven digits). Remember, there is a prescribed order to be observed in listing the reference, namely, zone, easting, northing (Think ZEN).

Practice a few times. Soon it will become second nature.

☞ Activity #16 ☞

Other Maps

In addition to the USGS map, which serves to specifically locate your site and relate it to other pertinent physiographic and cultural features, you will want to collect any local or specialized maps that may be available. Valuable maps often can be found in old county atlases or histories. Urban and rural plat sheets are often available at your local county engineer's office and are usually of nominal cost for a copy. Depending on where your site is located, you can expect to find any number of map sources. Collect them as you find them, for you can never be sure when one might turn out to be very helpful.

Local History

It is important, before beginning your actual fieldwork, that you find out as much as you can about the site. Scanning early written histories sometimes provides valuable clues to general land use if not specific information as to your actual site. Local libraries usually carry a few of these early books. Cities of any size usually have a published city directory in which all properties, commercial as well as residential, are listed by address and owner. This kind of specific information provides the key to unlocking other "doors of data." The early volumes of these directories, found in most main branch public libraries, often go back into the last century.

A city directory is set up in such a way that it includes—to cite its own title page—a "complete alphabetical list of the names of all inhabitants over 15 years of age (including the names of married women), business firms and incorporated companies; also special street directories, classified business directory, and miscellaneous record of city and county officials, churches, schools, secret societies, benevolent, literary, and other associations." Indeed, tons of information about a site and its social environment.

A general index leads into each user-friendly volume and gives the historical/archaeological researcher any number of access points. If you have an empty lot that has lain vacant for decades, you would simply go to the street directory section of your volume and look up the street on which your lot, or "site," is located. Match it with an address number, and you have the name of the resident (if it was a home) or the business, church, or whatever, that occupied it. Follow up the name by using the alphabetized list of names and you can find out where your occupant worked, what kind of business it was, and what specifically he or she did

Sample Youngstown City Directory Pages

LUMBER One Foot or a Million — **THE HELLER BROS. CO.** PHONE G-2211 — **Mill Work** Cabinet Work Sash and Doors

YOUNGSTOWN 1924 DIRECTORY 821

Massaro Margaret res 266 Carlton
Massaro Pasquale wks N Y C R R res 440 N Garland ave
Massaro Tony boilermaker res 440 N Garland ave
Massaro Wm J [Josephine M] bkpr Truscon S Co res 1132 Berkley ave
Massaroch Mrs Anna res 1153 Springdale Ave
Massaroch John wks Truscon S Co res 1153 Springdale ave
Massea Joseph [Rose] tailor res 206 N Prospect
Massey Josephine maid Savoy Hotel
Massey Walter T [Lula Belle] agent Natl L & A Ins Co res 224 W Wood
Massie Albert [Hattie] janitor res 331 E Rayen ave
Masso Andrew [Minnie] laborer res 1007 Star
Masso Antoinette student res 1007 Star
Masso Humbert salesman Yo Grocery Co res 15 Tacoma ave
Masson Charles [Jennie] contractor 426 Emerson place
Massonic Anthony [Sarah] wks City res 712 Lexington ave
Massonic Sarah E phone operator res 712 Lexington ave
Massullo Daniel [Anna] wks Truscon S Co res 1360 Grandview ave
Massullo James [Ella] barber 280 N Watt res 257 Emerald
Mastaslau George waiter rms Savoy Hotel
Masternard John painter rms 123 N Garland ave
Masters Frank W [Hermine C] sheet metal worker res 331 Belmont ave
Masters Mrs Ida C clerk Strouss- H Co res 556 Warren ave
Masters Michael [Anna] wks Gen F Co res 405 E Woodland ave
MASTERS OLAN B asst sec and treas Dudley-Brown-Wick Co res 464 Lora ave
Masters Wm J [Clara C] forman Rep I & S Co res 165 Regent ave
Masti William [Mary] labtoer res 245 Adams
Mastilak Joseph [Anna] wks Rep I & S Co res rear 239 Adams
Masto Ralph contractor res 225 Williamson ave
Mastodonna Anthony [Antoinette] fireman res 317 Byron
Mastopietro Anna res 316 Calvin
Mastopietro Anthony wks Yo S & T Co res 316 Calvin
Mastopietro Louis boilermaker res 318 Calvin
Mastopietro Lucian [Elizabeth] res 318 Calvin
Mastopietro Lucy res 316 Calvin
Mastopietro Rose res 318 Calvin
Mastoras Gust wks J Papakostakis res 314 E Boardman
Mastranestis Stephen [Zoie] coffee house 241 E Boardman res 1368 E Madison ave
Mastrantonio John [Elizabeth] bricklayer res 130 Fox
Mastrio Michael [Mary] laborer res 952 Emmet
Mastro Joseph [Caroline] laborer res 245 Emerald
Mastro Joseph [Philomena] wks Truscon S Co res 903 Bentley ave
Mastro Michael [Mary] wks Yo S & T Co res 2876 Rose
Mastrodonato Giovanni [Erminia] wks Yo S & T Co res 220 Emerald
Mastroianni Anna teller Union Savings Bank res 512 Parmelee ave

Sherwin-Williams Paints and Varnishes, Mirrors — **PAINT "Y" STORE** — Dry Colors, Oils Insecticides Glass

---

Ad-Letter Shop 122 S. Phelps St. — **ADDRESSING** "SAY IT WITH LETTERS" — **PHONE** 7-3172

Craven — STREET DIRECTORY — Cypress 75

CRAVEN	1242 Breosto T	" Kohut P
From 2454 W Federal	1238 Anzivino Mrs C	" Pupa W
Northeast (Northwest)	— Vacant	" Fedor J
☞ EAST SIDE	1218 Abrie T	430 Barnec J
19 Gatti Mrs A	1214 Modarelli R	" Schubert J
21 Famartino D	1208 Chito F	426 Kovalchik A
25 Vitale Mrs M	1206 Mirto J	424 Yaken J
" Fortunato R		" Matasich M
" rear Yennerelli P	**CRESCENT**	*Bridge begins*
" " Camperelli S	From 1173 W Rayen ave	448 Marovich W
123 Italian Hall	south (Northwest)	436 Soski J
27 Osiewicz J	☞ EAST SIDE	344 Teryk Mrs M
29 Puskacz J	*Dakota ave intersects*	342 Kelly W H
123 Butch S	523 Volk P	340 Ustanovski M
15 Tonda Mrs R	519 Mocyna P	338 Wilby A
131 Chastean R	501 Willas E	332 Phillips Mrs S
" Island J H	*StClair ave ends*	334 Hrinko W
" Hose M	1221 Hollas J	328 Hodar A
133 Smith J J	1225 Toth G	526 Senik P
190 Chappel H	*Central ave ends*	329 Sede B
192 Clemente A	323 Hudock J	322 Thomas J
" Pandone F	" Nemeth J	" rear Vacant
194 DeSabato A	*Manning ave ends*	320 Druga J
209 Micastro A	219 Evanko J	316 Kish M
215 Caster A	☞ WEST SIDE	310 Pilat A
1273 Laurie A	*Dakota ave intersects*	308 Hreco J
1271 Laurie F	534 Colmon R	226 Severene M
126 Simon J	532 Cecko S	
1249 Simeone A	530 Kutlik P	**CURRY PLACE**
1236 Camiloti J	528 Prokop O	From 2242 Ohio ave west
☞ EAST SIDE	526 Remias Mrs S	(N S)
20 Fagnano F	524 Mudry M	
" Ottieri L	522 Ratay C	**CUSTER AVE**
125 Popio W	518 Adam A	From 714 Elm west to
Milan begins	516 Kishan J	Belmont ave (Northwest)
39 Frasco A	514 Nemchek S	☞ NORTH SIDE
216 Bowel F	512 Sanders E T	216 Evans Mrs L M
220 Vacant	508 Fintor Mrs E	218 Hennessy Mrs M
1278 Bowel N	506 Sele S	220 McGinnis Mrs E
1274 Scarpine J	504 Magdich F	222 Craver J W
1270 Popio J	502 Gelencser G	226 Robison Mrs L
239 Yennerelli Mrs E	434 Dawson W	228 Ashton T R
1246 Christine N	" Gross S	230 O'Malley J T

Maxwell AND **Chrysler** — Motor Cars — SOLD BY THE GORDON MOTOR CO.

there, who his or her spouse was, and how many children over 15 he or she had (as well as their names).

In using the directory as a research tool, you simply move back year by year (the directory is published annually) until you come to the year when the address at your "lot" is occupied. This can be a great pre-excavatory research project for your students.

☞ Activity #17 ☞

Local Informants

Investigators at the scene of a crime always interview witnesses, who are considered primary sources of information. The same goes for the site investigator. Local informants (witnesses) can provide singularly important data to the archaeologist (investigator). Their information may even be more accurate than that of the written records. Oral histories, as these informational sources are called, are the accounts of people who have first-hand knowledge of the site goings-on. These are individuals who may remember your site when it contained a functioning social unit. They might give you solutions to a multitude of otherwise difficult-to-answer questions. What business was carried out there? How many people lived or worked there? What did the structure look like? What was it like inside, and so forth?

Having the youngsters devise questionnaires and question the informants will have, at least, a two-fold benefit. First, the actual devising of a reliable questionnaire will help the young students by giving them pause to re-examine their site hypotheses and, if necessary, to modify, strengthen, rethink, or add to them. Second, the actual handling of the interviews by the youngsters will help to develop skills in interpersonal communication and self-confidence.

A sample questionnaire can be found, with the activities and work sheets, at the end of this chapter.

Teachers can make as much of this aspect of pre-excavatory research as they wish. The research can be used supplementally—another potential source of data for interpreting the site—or it can play a more dominant educational role. Teachers could invite their informants to class and make a day of it, probing issues of the past that go beyond the boundaries of the site under investigation. Classroom magic is inevitable whenever the young meet the old in warm reminiscence.

PRE-EXCAVATION RESEARCH:

ACTIVITIES, WORK SHEETS, AND SAMPLE QUESTIONNAIRE

ACTIVITY NO. 11

Activity: Design a Recording Form

Subjects: Science, Social Studies, Language Arts, Art

Rationale: This activity will help to (1) promote an appreciation for what kinds of data are important to know; and (2) understand how to effectively record them for future use.

Objective: The students will demonstrate their awareness of what kinds of information are important enough to keep a record of.

Activity Preparation:

☞ Discuss with the class the importance of collecting data. Explain how it is important to carefully collect data while they are available, because they eventually may be lost. Using the detective analogy, demonstrate how the collection of *evidence* at the "scene of the crime" is often of critical importance to solving the "crime."

☞ Explain the differences between *quantitative data* (having to do with quantity, capable of being counted or measured) and *qualitative data* (having to do with nonmeasurable qualities, e.g., color, shape, etc.).

☞ Explain how *forms* can allow for the more efficient recording of data.

Activity:

☞ Break the class into groups of four and have each group give itself an archaeological name (Examples: "The Diggers," "Dirt Movers," "Mummies").

☞ See which group can come up with the most *useful* and *recordable* categories of information about the classroom.

☞ List the categories on the board and separate them into quantitative and qualitative groups.

☞ Give each group a few pieces of 8½" x 11" paper and straightedges or rulers and assign them the job of getting all of the data categories on two sides of the paper. Remind them to allow sufficient room for the wordier, descriptive categories and the site drawing.

☞ Exchange the team-developed samples and discuss.

☞ Create a form that combines the best qualities of the various group-developed ones.

ACTIVITY NO. 11

Materials Needed: 8½" x 11" paper
rulers or straightedges
pen or pencils

Vocabulary: evidence
quantitative data
qualitative data
forms

ACTIVITY NO. 12

Activity:	Filling Out Forms
Subjects:	Science, Language Arts, Art
Rationale:	This activity will help to promote (1) observational skills; and (2) an appreciation for the variety of information that is recordable.
Objectives:	The students will demonstrate their abilities to utilize a pre-made form in recording site data.

Activity Preparation:

☞ Discuss with the class the importance of recording information at an archaeological site. Explain how information can be irretrievably lost if not accurately recorded in a timely manner.

☞ Tell the students to each bring to school a blank form from home. Any kind of form will suffice (have a few on hand just in case). Acquaint the students with the kinds of information asked for.

☞ Show, through example, the differences between *quantitative* and *qualitative data*. Explain how teamwork is needed to record some kinds of data.

Activity:

☞ Divide the class into groups. Give each group a copy of the form that they, as a class, had previously devised for recording information about their classroom. Have available for use several 3-meter tapes and one 10-meter tape.

☞ Direct them as teams to carefully record the classroom information called for on the form.

☞ Compare the forms for accuracy and discuss the results.

☞ Ask the class if there are any ways that they would modify the forms in order to make them more effective.

Materials Needed:
various blank forms
Classroom Record Forms (previously made)
pens or pencils
3-meter tapes
10-meter tape

Vocabulary: quantitative data   qualitative data

ACTIVITY NO. 13

Activity:	Measuring Distance on Maps
Subjects:	Science, Geography, Social Studies, Math
Rationale:	This exercise will help to (1) acquaint students with the *USGS topographic map*; and (2) familiarize them with some of the map terminology.
Objectives:	The students will know how to identify the map *quadrangle* and to measure distances on the map using the map scale.

Activity Preparation:

☞ Using a topographic map (or topo sheet), point out its outstanding characteristics. Caution: Don't attempt to get too deep into the lower left-hand corner information—unless, of course, you have advanced students and a keen knowledge of the system—as this material is largely irrelevant to successful map use at almost every level.

☞ Explain map *scale* and how it works. Acquaint students with the three scales—two English system and one metric—at the bottom of the map sheet and, using a pair of dividers, show how they are employed to measure distances on the map.

☞ Point out the *quadrangle* name in the top-right and lower-right corners. Explain how it works as part of a larger system, and show the eight adjacent quadrangles marked in the map margins. Point out the town or city on the map that gave the quadrangle its name.

Activity:

☞ Divide the class into "mapping teams" and give each group a different topo sheet. Give students the opportunity to look them over and comment.

☞ Give each student two small (1" x 6") strips of white poster board, a ruler or straightedge, and either a sharp pencil or a fine-tipped felt pen. Ask each student to make a feet and kilometer scale identical to the ones at the bottom of the map. Have them double-check for accuracy.

☞ Pass out Quad/Scale Work Sheets and have individuals fill them out using their team map. Make sure all team members participate.

☞ Check and discuss the results.

61

ACTIVITY NO. 13

Materials Needed: topographic maps
dividers
pencils
fine-tip felt pens
rulers or straightedges
poster board strips
work sheets

Vocabulary: topographic map
topo sheet
English system
metric system
quadrangle
dividers
scale
kilometer

QUAD/SCALE WORK SHEET

Topographic maps are among the most accurate maps in common use. Understanding them is an important part of understanding how archaeologists do their jobs. The entire United States has been divided into quadrangles so that every spot in the United States can be precisely located.

1.   What is the quadrangle of the map you are using?

2.   What map (quadrangle name) is located directly north of yours? _____
      What is directly west? _____
      What quadrangle is located between the two? _____

3.   List the eight quadrangles that surround yours.
      1. _____   5. _____
      2. _____   6. _____
      3. _____   7. _____
      4. _____   8. _____

4.   Can you tell from your map if your quadrangle is heavily populated or not?
      How can you tell?

5.   There is a mile, feet, and meter scale on the map. Which sits at the very bottom?

Knowing the scale allows you to measure the distance between different points on your map.

6.   Using your homemade scale, what is:
      a. the closest distance in feet and meters between the very lower left-hand corner of your map
         and the nearest road? _____ feet; _____ meters.
      b. the length of the longest straight road on your map? _____ feet;
         _____ meters.

      Print your name in the space below.

      _____

7.   Using your scale, how long is your name in feet? _____ In meters? _____

ACTIVITY NO. 14

Activity: Map Reading

Subjects: Science, Social Studies, Geography, Math

Rationale: This activity will acquaint students with various characteristics of a topographic map.

Objectives: Students will be able to recognize various map features and their uses.

Activity Preparation:

☞ Separate the class into "mapping teams" and give each group a *topographic map*.

☞ Starting with the information on the bottom margin, explain a map's *legend* and what the various notations and symbols mean, for example, road classification, *quadrangle* location, scale, *contour interval,* and so forth.

☞ Show what rivers, streams and lakes, cities and towns, and human made structures look like on the map.

☞ Explain the brown contour lines. Describe how they allow the map reader to tell the site's altitude or distance above sea level. Explain contour interval and the way it relates to the difference in height between one line and the next.

☞ Be prepared to answer questions about the various notations, numbers, and symbols on the map.

Activity:

☞ Give each mapping team a *topo sheet* and put a pencil dot or "site" on each map. Give each student a Map Reading Work Sheet.

☞ Have the students, using the scales they made earlier (or dividers if scales are not available), fill out the Map Reading Work Sheet. Have team members compare results.

☞ Each mapping team presents to the class the characteristics of its site as determined from the map, discussing such things as nearest water, closest population center or road, site altitude, and so forth.

Materials Needed:
topographic maps	pre-made scales or dividers
pens or pencils	work sheets

ACTIVITY NO. 14

Vocabulary: topographic map   topo sheet
                quadrangle   legend
                scale   contour
                contour interval   altitude
                sea level   symbols

MAP READER'S WORK SHEET

Maps, especially topographic maps, can tell us a great deal about a place before we even get there. They can accurately tell us about the nearest river, lake, city or town, road, house, cemetery, or airport. They can also tell us how high above sea level the site is. They can, in fact, be read like books.

Using the "site" marked on your topo sheet, answer the following map reader questions.

1. In what quadrangle is your site located?

2. How far is it (in meters) from the nearest road?
   According to the map legend what kind of road is it?
   Does it have a name or route number?
   What is it?

3. Is your site in a heavily populated area?
   How do you know?

4. If you wanted to go fishing, how far would you have to walk (in meters)?
   What kind of body of water is it?
   Does it have a name?
   What is it?

5. What is the nearest town or city we would go to for help if we needed it?
   Is it a big town or city?
   How do you know?

6. Are there any railroads nearby?
   Which ones?

7. Is the county name anywhere on the map?
   If so, what is it?

8. How high above sea level (in feet) is your site?

9. How much of a height difference is there between each brown contour line?
   How do you know?

10. *BONUS!* If a lot of brown contour lines are very close together what does it mean?

11. *BONUS!* Does a flat area have a lot or a few contour lines?
    Explain.

66

ACTIVITY NO. 15

Activity:	Learning UTM
Subjects:	Science, Social Studies, Geography, Math
Rationale:	This activity will help students to understand the basics of the Universal Transverse Mercator system.
Objectives:	Students will be able to identify map symbols having to do with the Universal Transverse Mercator, or UTM, system.

Activity Preparation:

☞ Explain to the students how the entire world (with the exception of the polar caps) has been broken down into 1,000- x 1,000-meter squares measuring east and west along the equator and north and south from the equator. Hold up a poster board drawing of the globe criss-crossed with grid lines. Caution: Do not get too detailed as this is a very technical subject.

☞ Using a topo sheet, explain how the UTM system works. Show in the lower left-hand corner of the map how each map has a zone number.

☞ Discuss *easting*. Point out the light blue ticks and the easting numbers along the upper and lower map margins and explain what they mean.

☞ Discuss *northing*. Point out the blue ticks and northing numbers along the two side margins of the map and explain them.

Activity:

☞ Break the class up into "mapping teams" and give each group a topo sheet. Give teams a few minutes to orient themselves to their map.

☞ Hand out Understanding UTM Work Sheets, pre-made map rulers, (or, where needed, dividers) and have students fill them out.

☞ Discuss results.

Materials Needed:

topographic maps	map
rulers	teacher's poster of UTM
work sheets	UTM illustrations
pens or pencils	

Vocabulary:

UTM	equator
dividers	easting
northing	zone number

67

UNDERSTANDING UTM WORK SHEET

The UTM system breaks the world down into squares measuring 1,000 meters (or one kilometer) on each side. These are grouped into *zones* each measuring roughly 100,000 meters along each side and containing 10,000,000,000 square meters! Your site can be accurately located on the globe by carefully measuring in its UTM location.

What have we learned so far about the UTM system?

1. What is your map quadrangle?

2. What is the *zone* on your map?

3. Using your ruler or a pair of dividers, what is the distance between two of the blue ticks located along the map's edge?

4. How many *northing* numbers appear down the left-hand margin of your map?

   How many *easting* numbers appear across the bottom margin of the map?

5. In which *direction* do the *easting* numbers get steadily higher?

6. Think hard on this now. The *northing* numbers get higher as you go north on the map. That is because you are getting farther away from what?

7. What northing number fits between 4539 and 4541?

8. Which number is larger, the *easting* or the *northing*?

9. Using your ruler or straightedge, draw, on the back of the page, a square that, if it were on your map, would measure 1,000 meters on each side. Put a dot in it. How far from the bottom of your square (in meters) is your dot?

ACTIVITY NO. 16

Activity:	Measuring UTM distances
Subject:	Science, Social Studies, Geography, Math
Rationale:	This activity will help students to understand (1) the UTM system of mapping; and (2) how map measurements are made using it.
Objectives:	The students will be able to accurately locate and record specific UTM points (or "sites") on a topographic map.

Activity Preparation:	☞ Review what the students have learned about topo sheets up to now. Discuss UTM.
	☞ Using an overhead, show the class a UTM *coordinate counter* and carefully explain how it works.
	☞ Demonstrate the counter by locating and recording several "sites" on your topographic map. Take the time for extended questions and discussion.

Activity:	☞ Separate the class into "mapping teams" and give each team a topo sheet and yardstick or other long straightedge.
	☞ Give each student a UTM coordinate counter made from clear plastic and an instruction sheet.
	☞ On each topo sheet put a pencil dot for each team member.
	☞ Have the students specify the location of their individual sites and fill out a UTM Site Location Work Sheet.

Materials Needed:	topographic maps coordinate counter overhead clear plastic UTM coordinate counters yardsticks pens or pencils UTM Coordinate Counter Instruction Sheet work sheets
Vocabulary:	coordinate counter

COORDINATE COUNTERS

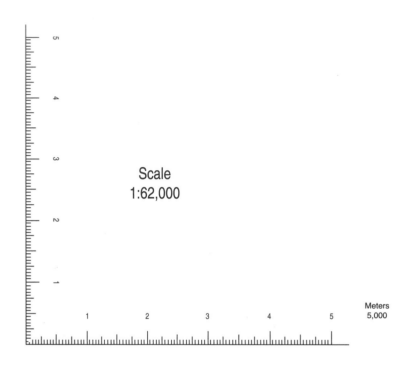

Scale
1:62,000

Meters
5,000

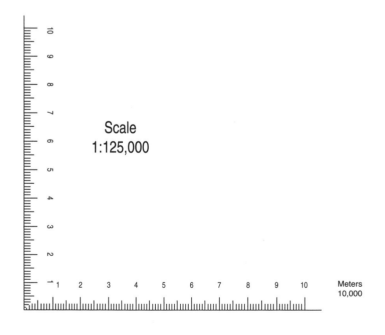

Scale
1:125,000

Meters
10,000

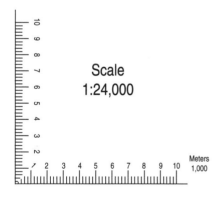

Scale
1:24,000

Meters
1,000

UTM SITE LOCATION WORK SHEET

Using the Universal Transverse Mercator system, or UTM as we call it for short, is an accurate and speedy way to locate and record points on a topographic map. The job has been made even easier with the invention of the clear plastic coordinate counter. With this tool, precise locations can be recorded in minutes.

Let's say you are an archaeologist who has been out in the field looking for important prehistoric sites that you may want to excavate. How would you use your mapping skills to tell someone else exactly where your site was located?

1. What is your map quadrangle?

2. What is your map's scale?

3. What is the date that your map was made?

4. How many blue UTM ticks are there running across the bottom margin of your topo sheet?

    How many running up the side margin?

5. Notice that on some maps, the entire easting and northing numbers can be found in the margins. How many digits are in the full easting number?

    How many are there in the northing?

Most of the time the *easting* consists of just three digits, like 525, and the *northing* just four, like 4619. These are incomplete values and are waiting for a map reader or archaeologist like yourself to supply the remaining three digits. Think of them as looking like this, 525_ _ _ and 4619_ _ _.

The teacher has marked an important archaeological site on your map. Tell us where it is using the UTM system.

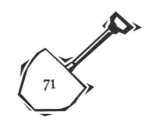

UTM SITE LOCATION WORK SHEET

SITE ONE (*Remember,* eastings have six digits total and northings have seven!)

Zone _____

Easting _____

Northing _____

Check with your teacher to see how well you've done.

Okay! Now that you have all the confidence of an Indiana Jones, have your teacher mark a second site on your map and have another go at it!

SITE TWO

Zone _____

Easting _____

Northing _____

HOW TO USE THE UTM COORDINATE COUNTER INSTRUCTION SHEET

For each point, or "site," to be measured follow these steps:

1. Write the *zone number* onto your work sheet.

2. Using your yardstick or straightedge, draw a line lightly from the top margin of the map to the bottom margin connecting the UTM ticks directly *west* (or left) of the site.

3. Draw a similar line lightly from the left margin of the map to the right margin connecting the UTM ticks directly *south* of (or below) the site. *This line will intersect the first line you drew somewhere southwest of your site.*

4. Copy onto your work sheet the portions of the easting and northing values given with the UTM ticks through which your lines were drawn. (*Hint: The easting values will be three digits and the northing will be four digits.*)

5. Using the scale on the coordinate counter that matches your map scale (usually this will be 1:24,000), line up the counter on the map so that:
   a. the side of the horizontal scale (the one that reads from *right to left*) lies along the east to west line; and
   b. the side of the vertical scale (the one that reads from left to right or down to up, if you want to think of it that way) passes directly through the site.

6. *Make sure you are lined up correctly!*

7. Read the scale right to left for the *easting* and upward for the *northing.*

8. Enter the values—it will be 3 digits for both the easting and northing, onto your work sheet. *Double check your readings!*

ACTIVITY NO. 17

Activity:	Who Lived There?: Using a City Directory
Subjects:	Social Studies, History, Language Arts, Geography
Rationale:	This activity will help the student to appreciate (1) primary historical research; and (2) how much can be learned from a standard city directory.
Objectives:	The students will be able to find and utilize the information contained in a city directory.

Activity Preparation:

☞ Discuss the importance of historic *research* to archaeology. Explain how learning about a site before digging it can help in the subsequent excavation and understanding of it.

☞ Show the class a copy of a local *city directory*. List some of the *index* subjects on the board and discuss what they mean.

☞ Randomly choosing a street address as your "empty lot," demostrate to the class all of those things you can learn from the directory. Write them on the board.

☞ Have the class make suggestions on other, less obvious, things that the directory might tell us.

Activity:

☞ Separate the class into research teams and give each group a volume of the city directory and a city street map.

☞ Have each group randomly select a city address as its hypothetical "empty lot" and, using the data provided by the city directory, gather as much information as it can about their site. Use the City Directory Work Sheet to record the data.

☞ See which group can make the most imaginative—but realistic— use of their directory. Compare results and discuss.

Materials Needed:

city maps	city directories
work sheets	pens or pencils

Vocabulary: research   city directory   index

Note: This classroom activity is feasible only if city directories are available to teacher and students; otherwise, a trip to the library is necessary.

THE CITY DIRECTORY WORK SHEET

As we've found out in class, lots of things can be learned about an archaeological site from an official *city directory* if the site is located within the limits of a city or town. Archaeologists do as much research as possible before going into the field because it can give them hints on what to look for and how to approach the actual excavation of their site.

For just a moment, put yourself in the role of a young and brilliant archaeologist. Assuming the city address that you selected is now an empty lot, what can the directory tell you that might not be so easy to learn just by digging?

1. What is the address of your empty lot?

2. Was it a residence or a business address?

   If it was a residence, answer the following questions to the extent that you can. If it was a business address, then answer questions 13 to 21.

3. Who is listed as the resident?

4. Was the resident married?

   If so, what was the spouse's name?

5. Were there any children over 15 living there?

   If so, what were their names?

6. Where did your site resident work?

7. Could he or she walk to work?

   How far was it? (blocks)

8. What kind of business or company was it?

9. What, specifically, was his or her job?

10. If there were children under 15 years of age, where would they have gone to school? (It will be the nearest school.)

THE CITY DIRECTORY WORK SHEET

11. What was the nearest church to your empty lot?

   What denomination was it?

12. What are some other things the directory might tell you about your empty lot archaeological site?

If your address was a business or company, answer questions 13 to 21.

13. What was the official name of the business?

14. What kind of business was it?

15. Who was the head (president or manager) of the company?

16. Did the business advertise in the city directory?

   If so, on what page?

17. If the business was incorporated, what year did its incorporation take place?

18. Where did the company head reside?

19. Was he or she married?
   If so, what was the spouse's name?

20. Did they have anyone living with them?

   Who?

21. What else can you tell us about the business that once occupied your now empty lot?

SAMPLE QUESTIONNAIRE

(For use in gathering information from local informants about lot use)

Information About the Informant
Informant Name:
Address:
Phone:
How long have you lived here?

About the Structure (Outside)
Do you remember the structure that stood on this lot?
How many stories high was it?
What was it made of (stone, brick, wood, etc.)?
Did it have a basement or cellar?
What color was it?
How was the door placed? The windows?
Was there a porch?
Was there anything unusual about the building?
Were there plants, flowers, shrubs, or trees surrounding it? If so, what?
What other things can you recall about the building?
If it was a business or something other than a residence, what was it?
What was its official name?
What kind of business was it?
Was it a busy place?

Inside the Structure
Were you ever inside the house?
How many rooms did it have?
Can you remember the layout of the rooms?
Was there anything unusual about the interior?

About the Residents or Site Users
Do you know the family's name?
How many adults lived there?
How many children lived there?
What were their approximate ages?
What was the gender of the children? How many boys? Girls?

SAMPLE QUESTIONNAIRE

Were there any pets? What?
Do you know what the family occupation(s) were?

Other Remarks or Comments

LAYING OUT THE SITE

The on-the-ground phase of archaeology begins with gridding off the site into manageable subunits. An entire lot, or structural ground plan, is usually too big to excavate as a single unit. It must be subdivided into smaller segments that, in turn, can be excavated efficiently by a three- or four-party team.

The gridding is actually done for two reasons. First, the use of the excavation grid is necessary to archaeological accuracy. The small units into which the site is divided gives the investigator tighter control of the excavation. Artifacts and specimens can be more accurately plotted according to their specific provenience, or location, within the site. Second, not only is the smaller unit more archaeologically sound, it is advantageous to both teacher and student. It is usual to have two youngsters doing the actual excavating while two others sift the soil through wire mesh table screens. A unit in excess of two-by-two meters is too large for most inexperienced youngsters to control. They seem to work better within close perimeters.

☞ Activity #18 ☜

Arbitrary or Nonarbitrary Units?

Common sense is called for in deciding on the grid layout. A lot measuring eight meters along each side would normally be broken down into a grid with 16 arbitrary and contiguous two-by-two units if there was no more logical or compelling reason to do otherwise. However, if the site were to consist of structural remains in which room separations or walls were visible to the eye, then it would make more sense to use real divisions, such as subunits, because they are not arbitrary, rather they reflect divisions wherein the collected material has a "truer" contextual meaning. In short, if real subdivisions exist, use them; if they do not, create artificial ones.

Gridding the Site (Arbitrary)

Gridding the site begins with the establishment of a datum point, datum line, and base line. The site grid is composed of a series of squares created by the intersecting of two sets of parallel lines. The distance between each line is determined by the archaeologist (teacher). As stated above, two-meter units seem to work best with sites of the sort you will be digging.

☞ Activity #19 ☜

To establish your grid you must first establish your *datum point*. This is the point from which all of your site measurements are taken. It is a good idea to locate your datum in such a way that the datum and base lines running off of it embrace the site in only one quadrant. This makes it easier to handle the grid coordinates.

ARBITRARY GRID UNITS (QUADRANT)

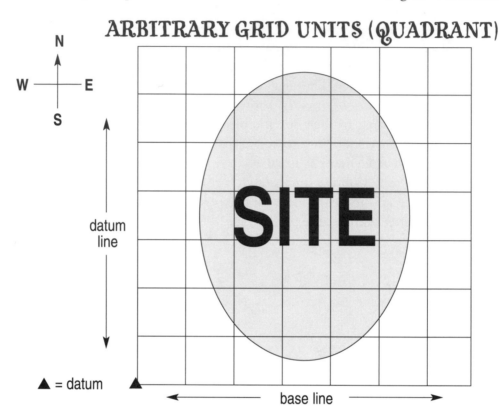

Once you've determined your datum, drive a 1" x 1" x 18" wooden stake into the ground to mark it. Next establish a *datum line* by running a length of mason's line or nylon string across the center of the stake (a nail driven into the top of the stake makes an efficient measuring point) in a north–south direction. *Most* arbitrary grids are laid out in a line with true north. This certainly is a good idea, particularly if there is no better reason for doing otherwise. But, if running the datum line in another direction is more logical—for example if the site itself is oriented in a different way—do it! Use a good pocket transit or surveying compass to ensure that the strings of your grid are in the proper alignment. The staked datum line should extend just beyond the limits of your site.

The base line intersects with the datum line atop the datum stake. The *base line* is created by running a line at 90 degrees to the datum line. Of course, if the datum line is north–south, the base line will be east–west. Again, this line is carefully laid in with a transit or surveying compass and should extend to just beyond the site perimeters.

At this point we have two stretched lines staked in place and intersecting at datum.

Now it's time to create our two-meter grid. From the datum point (use the nail), stretch a 30-meter tape tautly north along the datum line. Using a thick black felt

marker, tick the string carefully at two-meter intervals to a point just past the perimeters of your site. Repeat the same process south along the datum line and east and west along the base line. You are now ready to put down your grid strings that will frame your excavation units.

Next, cut a length of string and stretch it between two stakes. It should be about as long as the datum line. It will be laid parallel with and two meters away from the datum line. It takes four people to do this most efficiently. Two individuals hold the string taut and roughly parallel to the datum line; a third person, straddling the base line, aligns the stretched string with the first black tick (the two-meter mark); and the fourth person, standing near the north end of the string and using a small 3-meter tape, carefully measures two meters out from the datum line. The stakes are hammered into place. At this point you have two strings, exactly parallel, two meters apart.

Repeat the process at the four-meter tick, and so forth, eventually completing a series of staked lines parallel to the datum line and set at two-meter intervals. When this is done, repeat the same process along the base line. When you are finished, you have a site criss-crossed with a series of strings which forms a grid pattern of two by two units.

Once the grid pattern has been established you must decide on your grid designations. Keep it simple. There are all sorts of numbering, lettering, and combinatory systems used by archaeologists and each has its advantage in one way or the other. You can, if you wish, label each with a different letter. However, this necessitates getting into primes (A', B', C', etc.) or combining upper- and lower-case letters (Aa, Bb, Cc, etc.) if you have more than 26 units, and this can get cumbersome and awkward. For your project, a system should be used that numbers the ordinates (along the datum line) and letters the *abscissa* (along the base line).

> Ironclad Rule #5—Check and recheck measurements. An accurately laid-out grid is essential for precise records because all artifacts, specimens, and features unearthed within the grid pattern are described according to their position within a particular square.

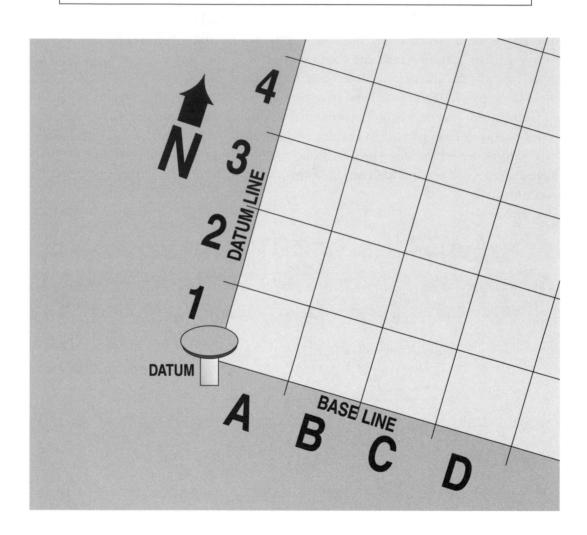

Gridding the Site (Nonarbitrary)

If the site you choose contains visible remains such as walls, floors, or features that define genuine functional units, it makes good sense to coordinate your system with these, more meaningful, context units. Let's say your chosen site is a recently razed and buried house foundation with remnants of its walls still visible above ground. It makes good sense to let these walls serve as your basic grid dividers. In doing so, you are helping to ensure a contextual integrity. For example, if your site contains four recognizable and discrete units of different size which, for the sake of argument, represent the living room, bedroom, bathroom, and kitchen, think how your recovered artifacts would be mixed together if you ignored the separation and excavated with a standard arbitrary grid.

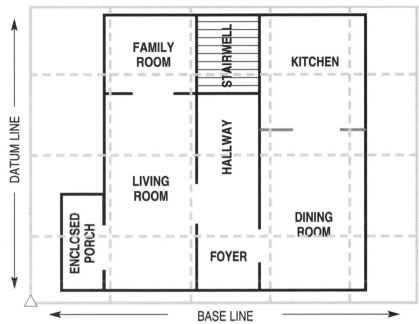

Notice how the arbitrary grid (light line) mixes material from different use areas (rooms).

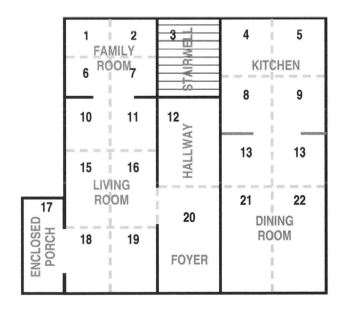

If the walls (dark lines) are visible then utilize them to separate units. That way you will not mix real areas (or rooms). The above demonstrates just one way it can be done. Each number represents a unit.

Your accuracy of interpretation improves greatly when you separate artifacts, observations, features, and so forth, that are culturally separated by architectural walls from each other. Kitchen artifacts go with kitchen artifacts, living room with living room, and so on. In short, artifacts and features that belong together should stay together. But what happens if the discernible, nonarbitrary units are too big to excavate as a single unit?

When a nonarbitrary unit is too large to handle comfortably, it can be broken down into smaller arbitrary subunits. A walled area four-by-four meters in size is easily divided into four two-by-two-meter units for more controlled digging.

With your grid in place, you're ready to dig!

Ironclad Rule #6—Do not become a slave to your methodology. Never forego accuracy, but always retain a methodological flexibility.

LAYING OUT THE SITE:
ACTIVITIES AND WORK SHEETS

ACTIVITY NO. 18

Activity:	The Classroom as Site
Subjects:	Math, Social Studies, Science, Art
Rationale:	This exercise will give the students a better understanding of (1) how and (2) why archaeological sites are mapped and gridded prior to excavation.
Objectives:	The students will use the metric system in measuring and mapping the classroom and the furniture in it.

Activity Preparation:

☞ Explain the importance of *provenience* and how critical it is that all of the site material is located as precisely as possible. Explain why site *gridding* must precede site excavation.

☞ Explain how scientists, including archaeologists, use the *metric system,* and give a demonstration using a 3-meter tape. Show how proper care should be taken of the tape.

☞ Discuss *unit* size. Establish that the size of each unit depends on the site being dug and on the needs of the people doing the work.

Activity:

☞ Separate the students into "mapping teams" and give each team a 3-meter (or 5-meter) tape, a piece of graph paper, and a ruler.

☞ Have the teams break the classroom down into a grid pattern of one-meter units and draw it to scale using the graph paper and rulers.

☞ Instruct the teams to plot in all of the classroom furniture as accurately as possible

Materials Needed:

3- or 5-meter tapes
graph paper
pens or pencils
rulers

Vocabulary:

grid
provenience
metric system
unit

ACTIVITY NO. 19

Activity: Gridding a Site (Arbitrary Units)

Subjects: Science, Social Studies, Geography, Math

Rationale: This activity will familiarize students with (1) how archaeological sites are gridded; and (2) the differences between arbitrary and nonarbitrary grids.

Objectives: Students will understand how an arbitrary grid is selected for a site and will know how to interpret it.

Activity Preparation:

☞ Explain why archaeological sites are broken into *grid units* prior to site excavation, reviewing such concepts as provenience, context, and so forth. Point out that archaeologists have a need to precisely record where artifacts came from, and the grid pattern allows them to do that.

☞ Explain the differences between an *arbitrary* grid—a grid not fixed by any set rules rather left to the archaeologist's judgment, and a *nonarbitrary* grid—a grid that is fixed by the logic of the site rather than the discretion of the archaeologist. Give examples of how each has its place.

☞ On the chalkboard, draw a plan view of a site. Place your *datum*— explaining what it is and the function it serves. Draw your north– south *datum line* through datum and explain. Draw your *base line* through datum and explain. Decide on a unit size and, measuring out from datum along both the datum and base lines, put in your units. [**Note:** Give at least two examples: one, when your datum originates outside the site perimeters and the site is located in a single *quadrant*, and second, when the datum itself is located within the site perimeters. Discuss the differences.]

☞ Discuss grid designations or labeling. Explain the commonly used two-meter grid system (in which units are labeled north–south and east–west from datum); the lettering system (in which each unit gets a different letter of the alphabet); and the combination number-letter system. Discuss the pros and cons of each.

Activity:

☞ Give each student an Arbitrary Grid Unit Work Sheet.

☞ On the chalkboard draw two large gridded sites—one with the site centered and one with the site located in a quadrant. Designate them along the datum and base lines only, using the two-meter grid system.

87

ACTIVITY NO. 19

Randomly place the following artifacts or symbols into different grid units on each of the two site maps: arrowhead, pot, sun symbol, teepee, tomahawk, and bone.

☞ On each of the students' two work sheet grids place one or two small stickers (or other mark of your choice).

☞ Students should complete their work sheets with reference to the chalkboard sites.

☞ Discuss the results.

Materials Needed: work sheets
pens or pencils
stickers

Vocabulary: grid
arbitrary grid
nonarbitrary grid
quadrant
datum
datum line
base line
unit

GRID UNIT WORK SHEET

We know that archaeologists must grid off their sites before they begin to excavate. The grid units in which the archaeologists will dig helps them to keep an accurate record of where artifacts and other "finds" come from. Exact location is an important tool for determining both artifact and site use.

There are lots of different ways to label a site once it is set up. Some have advantages in one situation, and some in another. It's up to the archaeologist in charge to make the final decision.

Let's see how well we remember what we learned about arbitrary grids!

In the first group of questions, the teacher is the head archaeologist and has decided on the grid labeling system. Using the teacher's unit designations, complete the following:

In the quadrant grid:
1. What unit is the arrowhead located in? _____
2. The pot? _____ 3. Tomahawk? _____
4. Teepee? _____ 5. Sun symbol? _____
6. Bone? _____

Good! Now let's try doing the same thing with the site-centered grid!
In the site-centered grid:
1. What unit contains the tomahawk?_____
2. The sun symbol? _____
3. Teepee? _____ 4. Arrowhead?_____
5. Pot?_____ 6. Bone?_____

On the attached grid plans (one quadrant and one centered), you are the head archaeologist (That's a lot of responsibility!), so you must label the grid system.

Label *both* grids using a system that works. Put a small triangle at your datum point and label along the datum and base lines.

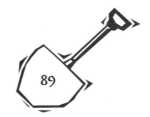

GRID UNIT WORK SHEET

ARBITRARY GRID UNITS (QUADRANT)　　　ARBITRARY GRID UNITS (CENTERED)

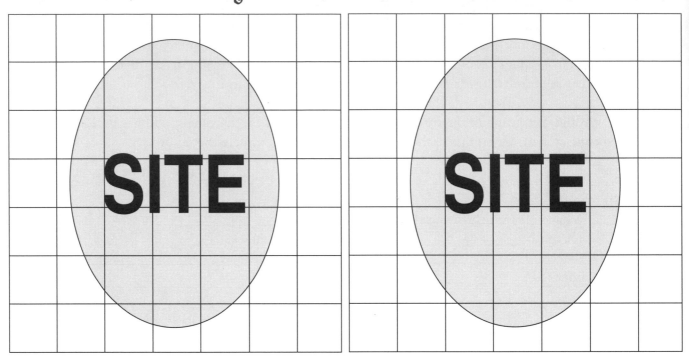

Look at the stickers or marks that the teacher put on each of your maps. In what units are they located according to your labeling system?

MAP ONE (QUADRANT)　　　　**MAP TWO (CENTERED)**

Sticker or Mark 1 _____　　Sticker or Mark 1 _____

Sticker or Mark 2 _____　　Sticker or Mark 2 _____

Congratulations! You are a site-gridder first class!

ACTIVITY NO. 20

Activity:	Gridding a Site (Nonarbitrary Units)
Subjects:	Science, Social Studies, Math, Geography, Art
Rationale:	This activity will familiarize students with the archaeologist's use of nonarbitrary units.
Objectives:	The students will understand when it is proper to grid an archaeological site using nonarbitrary units.

Activity Preparation:

☞ Review the difference between arbitrary and nonarbitrary units.

☞ Using several high-angle or *plan view* shots or drawings of sites or ruins taken from magazines or elsewhere, show the class how grids would be laid out taking advantage of what is known about the site or structure. Explain *plan view*—a view of a site taken from directly overhead.

☞ Draw on the chalkboard several different plan view outlines or floor plans and show how a workable and nonarbitrary grid can be superimposed atop it. Demonstrate how nonarbitrary units make use of real context units.

Activity:

☞ Have students bring a picture from home that is similar to the plan view or floor plan pictures shown in class.

☞ Using a fine-point black marker and a ruler, have them draw a workable grid atop their picture and label datum and the units.

☞ Pass out the Floor Plan of My House Work Sheet and have the students fill them out as directed.

☞ Discuss the results.

Materials Needed:

plan view pictures of structures or sites
fine-tip black marking pens   pens or pencils
rulers   work sheets

Vocabulary:

arbitrary unit   floor plan
nonarbitrary unit   grid
plan view

FLOOR PLAN OF MY HOME WORK SHEET

Remember: It's usually better to use a nonarbitrary grid pattern when you have a clue as to what lies below. It helps to keep things together that belong together. For instance, doesn't it make more sense to keep all of the kitchen stuff together rather than to mix it with the bedroom things? Sure it does.

First Floor

Draw a floor plan of the first floor of your home. Draw it as close to scale as you can and label all of the rooms. Don't forget hallways and deep closets. Put in permanent, or unmovable, fixtures like your stove, sink, and so forth.

Second Floor

Draw the floor plan of the second floor (if you have one) of your home. Do the same as you did for the first floor.

EXCAVATION

The most efficient unit excavation should involve four youngsters: two doing the actual digging and two working the nearby table screen. However, as with other methodological considerations, allow your own situation to be the deciding factor.

☞ Activity #21 ☞

The Grid Excavation Plan

As a general rule, do not excavate two adjacent squares or units at the same time. Instead, use a checkerboard pattern, digging alternate units in order. This ensures maximum coverage (or "uncoverage") with minimal digging. Since most of the sites you are likely to excavate are relatively confined in area, you probably have no need to get any more elaborate than this. Larger, more complex archaeological sites, of course, entail more extravagant methodologies such as trenching and level stripping.

An important part of your pre-excavation planning involves choosing the best location for your screening stations and backdirt pile(s). The primary consideration here is to locate your screens and backdirt pile in an area that, in all likelihood, will never be excavated, preferably off the site itself. This way, you will not waste valuable time—and your young diggers' patience—picking up "old" dirt and moving it again. Among archaeologists, moving backdirt and refilling holes is the stuff of which Purgatory is made and, though some claim it is good for the soul, teachers can probably find better ways to utilize their instructional time. Although you are trying to keep backdirt off the area to be excavated, you must try to keep it as close to where you are digging as possible. This obviates the need to move the dirt too great a distance from shovel to screen. Keeping the dirt close-by also makes backfilling at the close of excavations much less troublesome.

Controlled Surface Pick-Up

After you grid and string off your site, and before your actual digging begins, you will want to carry out what is often called a *controlled surface pick-up*. This procedure involves your students systematically going over every square inch of the gridded site and picking up *everything* cultural or man-made within the confines of each unit. Again, you pick up *everything!*

The value of such a systematic surface search on archaeological sites is three-fold. First, it removes surface artifacts that might, in time, be picked up by site visitors or otherwise destroyed by natural phenomena. Second, determining the relative density of artifacts in each part of the site might help indicate the relative density of the arti-

facts buried in the areas below the surface. A dense concentration in one area of your grid, for instance, could mean a similar concentration below, thereby giving you a better idea of which units to dig first. Third, and this is related somewhat to the second, the concentration of materials of a related use or function in one area of the site might provide clues to help interpret the activities that were carried out there—and in the area below. Retain material collected this way in a bag with the unit designation and the word "surface" written on it.

Of course, much of the surface material may not in any way relate to the site itself or to the activities taking place there. Much of your carefully collected "artifacts" may be modern rubbish dumped there well after the site's abandonment and subsequent burial—some, perhaps, even just hours before you've arrived to dig. Nevertheless, clearing the site of this noisome material provides a valuable service and prepares your site for excavation.

☞ Activities #22 & #23 ☜

Moving the Dirt

The most commonly used excavating tools are the shovel, trowel, whisk broom, dust pan, and *gloves*. Make sure *all* the youngsters are wearing gloves; sharp pieces of glass commonly abound in sites of the sort you are digging. The shovel is used primarily to remove a bulk of the site overburden. The *overburden* is the dirt fill which lies over and around your artifacts and features. However, when artifacts and features begin to appear, shift from shovel to trowel and whisk broom. The delicately manip-

ulated trowel is more forgiving of error than the awkwardly wielded shovel. The important thing is to know when to make the switch. Youngsters will tend to prefer the trowel because it is less physically demanding and because they can use it in a comfortable sitting or kneeling position, but you move far less dirt with a trowel than you do with a shovel. It pays to remind your young charges of the direct and positive correlation between the number of things you find and the volume of dirt you move. In general, practice will teach you when one tool is more appropriate than the other.

Place the excavated soil in plastic buckets and carry it to the nearby table screen to dump it for sifting. Youngsters with trowels and *gloves* should push the soil through the screen and retain the artifacts and other specimens which are caught. You must be careful at this stage not to mix material from different units. Usually the shoveling goes much faster than the screening, causing a backlog where the screeners are working frantically while the shovelers are standing about waiting to empty their buckets. You can remedy this by shifting some of your diggers to the screen. The whole idea is to create a steady flow where everyone is moving at just the right pace. As you become accustomed to the "rhythm" of the site, you can move people about for maximum effectiveness.

☞ Activity #24 ☜

The Artifact Bags

Each unit has at least two bags associated with it. Keep one in the unit where you place all the artifacts and specimens recovered by the diggers. Keep the other by the screeners, who will use it to hold the artifacts they discover during the sifting phase. It is important to label each bag properly in order to maintain accurate provenience. On a genuine archaeological site the typical bag labeling would include the official site designation, the specific unit in the site from which the artifacts came, the specific level or depth in the unit, the date, and the name or initials of the unit excavators.

The official site "name" is a trinomial designation consisting of a one- or two-digit number followed by two letters followed by another number. For example, "33 MH 21" is a site designator which tells us that the site is located in Ohio (Ohio is the 33rd state alphabetically) in Mahoning County (MH is the state's abbreviation for Mahoning County), and was the 21st site officially recorded for that county. In your case, use the actual state and county designation for your site—you can get this information by phone from your state's historic preservation office (SHPO)—and create your own specific site number, maybe by tacking on your homeroom number. You might also invent your own designating system, using your youngsters' talents in yet another way.

⌲ **Activity #25** ⌲

Write the specific unit and level in the site in a form such as "Unit 1A-2," which represents, in this case, grid unit 1A, stratigraphic level 2. Put the date on the bag along with the initials of the excavators, so the dig supervisor then knows who to see if any questions arise. As you process your findings back at the classroom, which will serve as a cataloging station, add a *field specimen number* to each bag. This is the number given to the entire batch of artifacts coming from the same unit and level. More will be said about this number under the chapter on labeling and cataloging. The teacher would be wise to appoint a "specimen supervisor" whose responsibility in the field is to see that all of the bags are properly labeled and collected at the end of each dig day.

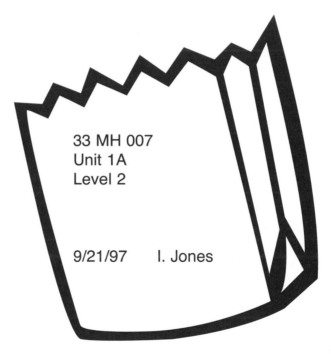

Vary the Site Jobs

Excavation of most sites using student help is a two-fold proposition. First you must always dig with an eye toward the accurate retrieval of data. Dig supervisors have the responsibility of ensuring that their crew can handle the various aspects of data recovery in a scientifically acceptable manner. However, the teaching aspect is also important. At one time or another, every archaeologist faced with a tight time schedule or a funding problem has to decide whether to focus on the site (and put the best diggers in the most important areas) or to emphasize the teaching (and put students into specific jobs without regard to their skills because they need the educational experience).

Since the elementary or secondary school archaeological projects we envision are decidedly educational and we specifically choose sites of no archaeological significance, teachers should make every effort to move youngsters into a wide variety of tasks. Students with exciting jobs must relinquish them after a time so that others may gain some experience. Similarly, youngsters excavating in units where artifacts occur in great numbers should expect to take their turn in pits less densely populated. The idea is to develop a broad spectrum of field skills in each of the youngsters.

An important part of any archaeological experience is the development of proper motor skills. Working with a variety of tools under a variety of situations helps students develop self-confidence around tools. Skill in using tools translates to a healthy regard for their proper and safe use and an appreciation of the care they require.

EXCAVATION:
ACTIVITIES AND WORK SHEETS

ACTIVITY NO. 21

Activity:	Excavation Techniques
Subjects:	Science, Social Studies, Language Arts
Rationale:	This activity will help the students appreciate the care that goes into the recovery of archaeological data.
Objectives:	The students will observe professional excavation techniques in practice and learn why these techniques and procedures are followed.

Activity Preparation:

☞ Show a film or slide group (See Appendix A) that demonstrates some of the common procedures used in *archaeological excavation* and the rationale for their use.

☞ Make a list on the chalkboard of the various *techniques* being utilized in the film or slides.

Activity:

☞ Give an Excavation Techniques Work Sheet to each student and instruct the students to fill them out.

☞ Have an open and in-depth discussion about the questions, covering any other points not raised.

Materials Needed:
excavation film or slides
work sheets
pens or pencils

Vocabulary:
archaeology
techniques
excavation

100

EXCAVATION TECHNIQUES WORK SHEET

Having just seen professional archaeologists at work, it is time for us to discuss the reasons for some of the techniques that we observed them use. You can be sure they had good reasons for the things they did. What were some of them?

1. When archaeologists get close to where the artifacts are located, they switch from using shovels to trowels and brushes. *Why?*

2. Did you notice that the dirt dug in each unit was sifted through a screen? *Why?*

3. Near each archaeologist was a small paper bag. *What was its function?*

4. When the archaeologist found an artifact or an important specimen, it was measured in place without moving it (called *in situ*). *Why?*

5. What do you suppose went into those notebooks laying near each unit? *Why?*

6. Why are the cameras important?

ACTIVITY NO. 22

Activity: Playground Pick-Up (Phase I)

Subjects: Social Studies, Science

Rationale: This activity will acquaint students with (1) controlled surface pick-up techniques; and (2) what they can learn from them.

Objectives: The students will understand how and why archaeologists carry out surface pick-ups prior to excavation by doing the same thing with the school playground.

Activity Preparation:

☞ Explain how the *artifacts* found in one area of a site can help reveal what specific activities occurred there. Explain how the volume of material recovered in one area reflects the amount of activity taking place there. Discuss the importance of accuracy in the recording of finds.

☞ Help the students visualize the school grounds as a site and discuss the various activities that occur there. What would one expect to find in those *activity areas*?

☞ Describe the technique called *controlled surface pick-up*, in which archaeologists systematically inspect the entire surface of a site prior to digging and record all of the materials they find, giving them a clue as to what may lie below.

Activity:

☞ Give each student a handful of spray-painted (fluorescent) Popsicle sticks (or surveyor's flags, if you have them).

☞ Line the students up side-by-side, at four-foot intervals (adjust interval for the class size or extent of the area to be picked up).

☞ Direct them to walk to the opposite side of the pick-up area and carefully inspect the ground in front and to the sides of them as they advance. When they find *any* piece of litter (an "artifact") they should flag it with a bright Popsicle stick *but should not pick it up*.

☞ Have them go back and forth across the area until they cover it completely. Point out any observable clusters of markers or any other noticeable anomalies.

☞ Have the students, working in small teams, make a sketch map on graph paper. Have them carefully plot each Popsicle-stick marker.

⌇⌇⌇⌇⌇⌇⌇⌇⌇⌇⌇⌇⌇⌇⌇⌇⌇⌇⌇⌇⌇⌇⌇⌇⌇⌇⌇⌇

ACTIVITY NO. 22

⌇⌇⌇⌇⌇⌇⌇⌇⌇⌇⌇⌇⌇⌇⌇⌇⌇⌇⌇⌇⌇⌇⌇⌇⌇⌇⌇⌇

Using a permanent, felt-tip marker, number each stick and put the number on a plastic sandwich bag to store each "artifact." Have them remove the Popsicle stick markers as they log each artifact.

☞ Put the bagged and numbered artifacts into a large trash bag or carton and return to class for later processing (Phase II).

☞ Discuss why clusters of artifacts appear in some areas and few appear in others.

Materials needed: Popsicle sticks
fluorescent spray paint (bright)
plastic sandwich bags
permanent, felt-tip markers
trash bag or cardboard carton
graph paper
clipboards
pens or pencils

Vocabulary: activity area
artifacts
controlled surface pick-up

ACTIVITY NO. 23

Activity:	Playground Pick-Up (Phase II)
Subjects:	Social Studies, Science, Language Arts
Rationale:	This activity will continue to familiarize students with the usefulness of a controlled surface pick-up as a pre-excavation technique.
Objectives:	The students will identify, classify, and determine the significance of artifacts recovered during the controlled surface pick-up of their school playground.

Activity Preparation:

☞ Review the surface pick-up which led to the recovery of the artifacts in the trash bag or carton. Discuss the procedure and what the students learned from it.

☞ Transpose the data from the graph paper plots to a larger grid on the chalkboard or large poster board. Discuss any anomalies. [**Note:** It might be better to prepare the transposition yourself before the discussion in order to save time, although doing it in front of the class might have its own value. You decide.]

☞ Discuss *classification* and how artifacts are grouped together by similarity of use or purpose. Bring some examples from home of things that go together like kitchen implements, toys, jewelry, car items, and so forth.

Activity:

☞ Divide the bagged artifacts among the students and have them clean the items.

☞ Have the students number each artifact directly (with a fine-tip marker) or with a small, numbered stick-on tag. Make sure the number matches the bag it came from.

☞ Have the students identify all of the items possible and group similar items together.

☞ Have the students fill out the Playground Pick-Up Work Sheet.

☞ Discuss results.

Materials Needed:

poster board	stick-on tags
fine-tip felt pens	work sheets
pens or pencils	

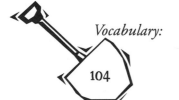

Vocabulary: classification

104

PLAYGROUND PICK-UP WORK SHEET

You have collected lots of different things from your playground. We might call them litter. But remember, yesterday's litter is today's artifact. Actually, archaeologists study litter that was dropped centuries ago.

We also learned that some areas of our playground contained more litter/artifacts than other areas did. Some areas also had different kinds of artifacts. Why?

See what you can do with these questions:

1. What artifact was the most commonly found? *Why?*

2. What part of your playground had the most "artifacts"? *Why?*

3. Could you tell by just the materials you picked up in a certain area what activity went on there? *How?*

4. If you were going to dig and look for artifacts underground, is there a place in your playground where you might look first? *Why?*

ACTIVITY NO. 24

Activity: Table Top Archaeology

Subjects: Science, Social Studies, Language Arts

Rationale: This activity will help familiarize students with (1) the basic elements of site excavation; and (2) accurate record keeping.

Objectives: The students will understand how careful excavation of each individual site unit results in a successful understanding of the whole site.

Activity Preparation:

☞ Review how archaeologists divide sites into smaller units so they can keep tight control of each artifact's place of origin (provenience) and *in situ* context.

☞ Discuss stratigraphy and how it helps the archaeologist to date items relative to one another. Review the law of superposition and its importance in site interpretation.

☞ Demonstrate how artifacts represent different activities. Provide examples.

☞ Prepare several (at least six) rectangular, plastic wash basins (or large, deep, disposal aluminum roasting pans) of identical dimensions as site units. Fill each container ("unit") with three distinct levels (use sand, potting soil, and kitty litter, for instance). In *each* level, place different artifacts—use small items like dish shards, bobby pins, paper clips, soda tabs, bones, and so forth. Make sure there is a stratigraphic consistency from unit to unit and put artifacts together that are associated with the same activity.

☞ Place the containers side by side on a table forming a complete "site."

It should look like this:

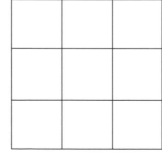

106

ACTIVITY NO. 24

Activity: ☞ Separate the class into "dig teams" according to the number of "units" available and give *each team* a kit consisting of two spoons, graph paper, sandwich bags, a felt-tip marker, a ½" paint brush, an index card, and work sheets.

☞ Have the class, *as a group*, determine a grid system and label each individual unit accordingly.

☞ Instruct each "team" to select a unit and tape an index card to the side of it with the unit designation printed on it.

☞ Have each team return to its work area with its unit container, cautioning the students not to disturb the contents as they move the containers.

☞ Each digging team will carefully excavate its unit, one level at a time, recording all observations and carefully separating and recording the artifacts.

☞ Give each student a Table Top Archaeology Work Sheet to fill in.

☞ *Each team* will present a summary of its unit findings to the class.

☞ The class (with the teacher's help and coaching) will reconstruct the "site."

Materials Needed: plastic basins or aluminum pans
kitty litter
potting soil
sand
index cards
spoons
felt-tip markers
graph paper
pens or pencils
½" paint brushes
sandwich bags
work sheets

Vocabulary: provenience
in situ
law of superposition
stratigraphy
levels
interpretation

TABLE TOP ARCHAEOLOGY WORK SHEET

1.   What is your unit designation?

2.   How many levels did you have?

3.   How many total artifacts did you find?
List them:

       a._____   b._____

       c._____   d._____

       e._____   f. _____

       g._____   h. _____

       i. _____   j._____

       k._____   l._____

       m._____

4.   Which level had the most artifacts in it?

5.   Were any of your artifacts associated with similar activities?
What were they?

6.   What did you learn that might help you when you dig a real site?

Hands-On Archaeology

ACTIVITY NO. 25

Activity:	Labeling Unit Bags
Subjects:	Science, Social Studies, Geography
Rationale:	This exercise will acquaint students with the importance of proper labeling of the unit bags and how the bag designation is determined.
Objectives:	Students will know how to label a unit field specimen bag properly and will understand the logic behind it.

Activity Preparation:

☞ Explain the *trinomial system* used by archaeologists throughout the United States and Canada. Explain how the first number represents the state (its alphabetical order), the two letters are the abbreviation for the county within the state, and the last set of numbers represents the official recording number of the site. Give examples. Display a large poster board with all of the state numbers listed.

☞ Discuss the importance of *uniformity* in science. Explain the need to eliminate confusion and error.

☞ Using an atlas of North America, show how states are all broken down into counties (or, in the case of Louisiana, by *parishes*).

☞ Explain how and why the site unit designation and stratigraphic level are the most important part of the bag label.

☞ Discuss the field specimen number and how it represents all of the artifacts and specimens contained in one bag.

Activity:

☞ Give each student a paper lunch bag and a felt-tip marker.

☞ Assign each student a *different* site location in a big city in one of the 50 states. (The students will have to use the atlas to determine their county.)

☞ Have the students label their bags accordingly, making up their unit designations and stratigraphic levels, and signing each bag. Collect the bags and discuss.

Materials Needed:	atlas of North America paper lunch bags	poster board felt-tip markers
Vocabulary:	trinomial system parish	uniformity county

109

MAINTAINING FIELD RECORDS

Artifacts retrieved from a site are easy to transport back to the classroom or laboratory for later description and analysis. However, this is not so with the important non-artifactual data such as stratigraphy and horizontal context or artifactual material like walls, floors, and chimneys, which are too large and cumbersome to remove. You must leave these in the field and take away only recorded information on them. The most efficient and accurate way to do this is by recording on specially prepared forms.

Forms are easy to design and can be custom-made to the type of site you happen to be digging. Letting the students help design the forms can also be an important part of the learning process. Site forms serve two very important functions. First, their relative brevity allows recording of a maximum amount of data in a minimum amount of time. Second, the visual form with its slots and blanks to fill in constantly prods the recorder (student) into becoming scientifically observant. A larger section labeled "Remarks" or "Comments" allows the imaginative or especially keen observer to add information not specifically asked for. Forms also provide structure which is useful for entering the information into a computer database.

Specific Forms

Encourage students to work together on the creation of forms specially designed for the site you are working on. Deciding what is important enough to be recorded is what critical thinking is all about. The various forms archaeologists currently use are the evolutionary product of years of use and individual modification. You probably need a minimum of four field forms during the excavation of an average site. These will be illustrated and discussed in turn. You can find a more complete sampling of potentially useful forms in Appendix B.

Historic Artifact Discard Sheet

This sheet was designed for use with archaeological sites containing a fair amount of surface debris which, while artifacts in the broadest sense of the term, nonetheless, is intrusive (i.e. not an actual part of the site) and, therefore, not significant archaeologically. Most lab facilities are limited in storage space and, of course, archaeology by its very nature is a "cumulative" science—that is to say, archaeological collections grow steadily bigger over time. There is constant pressure to unload the archaeologically irrelevant. However, it is a simple matter to keep a written record of what you are "unloading"—just in case. The form is for use in the field as well as back in the lab (classroom).

The Discard Sheet pretty much speaks for itself. It has slots for the site designation, field specimen (FS) number, location in the site (what unit), and depth (or stratigraphic level). The column marked *Description* allows you to describe what it is you are discarding. For instance, it might say, "White plastic ice cream spoon"; *Quantity* tells you how many: "2"; and *Comment* allows you to add any other observation you think pertinent: "Has words Dairy Queen imprinted on handle." This form, like all of the others, is 8½" x 11" in size and is designed for easy duplication and ready inclusion in a three-ring binder.

☞ Activity #26 ☞

The Feature Form

During the excavation process, anything unusual can be labeled a *feature*. Most features, in contrast to artifacts, which are highly portable, constitute the kind of evidence of past cultural activity which, for one reason or another, cannot be removed intact or transported back to the laboratory for study. One might call them "nonportable" artifacts because they must be examined and recorded only in the field.

A specially devised form facilitates the recording of essential data regarding the surface or subterranean features of a site. Number features sequentially *as you record them.* The form has slots for the site designation and the unit (or units) in which the feature occurs. An explanation of the entries, arranged by their numbers, follows:

(1)   *Definition*—Name, type, and identification (if possible) of the feature.

(2a)   *Location* (Horizontal)—The coordinate location in meters and centimeters.

(2b)   *Location* (From Surface)—Actual depth from the surface directly above the feature. If the feature itself has a thickness, note whether your measurement is to the top, bottom, or midpoint of the feature.

(3a), (3b) *Dimensions* (Length and Width)—The maximum length and width of the feature with direction (i.e. north-south, northeast-southwest, etc.).

(3c)   *Vertical Thickness*—The vertical distance taken between the uppermost and lowest points in the feature.

(4)   *Fill*—Description of the soil and other materials contained immediately in, over, and around the feature.

(5)   *Preservation*—Description of the state of preservation of the feature (poor, fair, good, collapsed, etc.).

(6a)   *Associations* (Features)—Itemization and brief description of other features which may be in association—connected in some way—with this feature.

(6b)   *Associations* (Specimens)—A similar itemization of any artifacts or specimens in association with your feature.

(7)   *Remarks*—Further observations as needed. You continuously add to this entry as you learn more about the feature. In some cases it may go on for pages.

At the bottom of the page is a place for the date and names of the recorders. The reverse side of the Feature Form is designed like graph paper, making it easier to add sketches and scale drawings if desired. This also allows the continuation of remarks or other data from the obverse side.

☞ Activity #27 ☜

Artifact Data Sheet

The primary function of this sheet is to record any significant artifacts you find *in situ* (Latin for "in its original place"). What constitutes "significant" is, of course, the archaeologist's call. Some sites might have so many artifacts per unit that pausing to fill out an Artifact Data Sheet for each one would leave no time for digging. Some archaeologists ignore them completely, finding that such detailed locational information on each artifact constitutes, for the most part, spurious precision.

On your dig you may make some "special" artifactual find that demands special recording. If so, use the form. The forms are also valuable teaching tools because they give students—and professionals, for that matter—pause to reflect about their site and their course of action.

The following is an explanation of some of the entries:

A. *Depth*—Actual depth from the surface directly above the artifact.
B. *Location*—Number of inches or centimeters south and east of the northwest corner of your unit.
C. *Scale*—Check the slot which matches your grid size.
D. *Map Location*—In the grid, mark the location of the artifact being recorded. Also mark any associated artifacts or features. You can also put measurements on the grid.
E. *Sketch*—Draw the artifact, highlighting outstanding or unusual characteristics, if any.
F. *Artifact Description*—Name, type, and identification (if possible) of the artifact. Be as complete as you need to be.
G. *Associations*—Itemization and brief description of any other artifacts or features that may be in association.
H. *Preservation*—Description of the state of preservation of the artifact *and* any curatory "first-aid," such as glue, that you apply to it.
I. *Remarks*—Further observations as needed.

Again, while it may be too burdensome to have students fill out one of these Artifact Data Sheets for every shard of broken glass or every rusty nail, it is still a good idea to have each of them do a few just for the valuable learning experience.

Activity #28

Universal Data Form

Many archaeologists prefer this form because of its ultimate flexibility; they can use it to record all manner of site information. It is included here so that teachers can have the opportunity to enjoy the same advantages. Its most obvious disadvantage, however, is that it leaves more to the observational powers of the excavator—in other words, it lacks the specific slots so convenient for jogging one's memory.

The following is an explanation of some of the less obvious entries:

A. *Definition*—A definition and description of what it is you are recording, that is, artifact, stratigraphy, feature, and so forth.

B. *Associations*—Itemization and brief description of anything which might be associated with the recorded item.

C. *Grid*—Use it to draw the feature, unit, artifact, and so forth, that you are recording.

D. *Observations*—Make observations you consider pertinent here.

The Continuation Sheet

This sheet is really no more than an 8½" x 11" piece of graph paper. Herein lies its utility: it can be used as the continuation sheet for any of the other forms, the graph paper making it equally good for both written notes and drawings.

Appendix B has a broad sampling of forms you may use as is or modify to fit your individual needs. And remember the previous discussion of the pros and cons of formal notes versus "freehand" ones: they both have their place. Do what works best for you. Let the forms add to the learning experience, not detract from it.

MAINTAINING FIELD RECORDS:
ACTIVITIES

ACTIVITY NO. 26

Activity:	Recording the Throwaways
Subjects:	Social Studies, Science, Language Arts
Rationale:	This exercise will familiarize students with the importance of record forms.
Objectives:	The students will know how to fill out a *Historic Artifact Discard Sheet.*

Activity Preparation:

☞ Discuss the importance of *forms* in archaeological record keeping.

☞ Using a poster board replica of a *Historic Artifact Discard Sheet,* explain the various columns and designations. Discuss.

☞ Carefully explain the meaning of the *field specimen* (or FS) *number.* The field specimen number is the number given to the entire batch of artifacts and specimens coming from *the same unit and level*—in essence, all of the contents of one bag.

☞ Tell how an archaeological site often contains *intrusive* artifacts which are not as significant as others—such as an empty cigarette pack or soda bottle left sitting atop a prehistoric mound by some modern hiker—and how they may be systematically recorded but then discarded. Explain how *repositories* have limited space and must be somewhat selective in what they preserve.

Activity:

☞ Divide the class into recording teams and give each team a wastebasket with trash in it taken from a different room in the school and a *Historic Artifact Discard Sheet.*

☞ Assuming each wastebasket is a unit bag, record *all* of the discarded material on the *Historic Artifact Discard Sheet.*

☞ Compare results and discuss.

Materials Needed:

poster board	wastebaskets (with refuse)
pens or pencils	Historic Artifact Discard Sheets

Vocabulary:

forms	records
field specimen number	intrusive
repository	

116

ACTIVITY NO. 27

Activity:	Recording Features
Subjects:	Social Studies, Science, Language Arts, Math
Rationale:	This exercise will familiarize students with the importance of record forms.
Objectives:	Students will know how to fill out a Feature Form.

Activity Preparation:

☞ Discuss *features*. Explain how they differ from artifacts *per se* and how, because of their lack of portability, they cannot be brought back to the laboratory (or classroom) like artifacts and other specimens.

☞ Using a poster board replica of a Feature Form, explain the various slots and categories of information the form calls for. Discuss *preservation* state and *association* with other features or artifacts. What significances are there? Elicit questions and discuss.

☞ Demonstrate the use of a *compass* to determine direction. Give students some practice (with guidance) in proper compass use.

Activity:

☞ Divide the class into recording teams and give each team a compass, a clipboard, 3-meter tape, and a Feature Form.

☞ Take the class outside the building and have each group select a different "feature" to record (e.g. jungle gym, manhole, Dumpster, etc.) using their form. If you decide to stay in the classroom, you can use various pieces of furniture as your mock features.

☞ Have each team record their "feature" as accurately as possible on their Feature Form.

☞ Compare results and discuss.

Materials Needed:

poster board	Feature Forms
pens or pencils	3-meter tape
compass	

Vocabulary:

features	preservation
association	compass

117

ACTIVITY NO. 28

Activity:	Recording Artifacts
Subjects:	Social Studies, Science, Math, Art, Language Arts
Rationale:	This exercise will familiarize students with the importance of record forms.
Objectives:	Students will know how to fill out an Artifact Data Sheet.

Activity Preparation:

☞ Explain how the recording of *artifacts* or *ecofacts* while *in situ* can be an important tool in archaeological work.

☞ Using a poster board replica of an Artifact Data Sheet, explain the various slots and categories of information called for. Walk through the form, discussing how archaeologists gather the information.

Activity:

☞ Give each student an "artifact" (something unusual from home or school—the more uncommon the better) and an Artifact Data Sheet.

☞ Along with each artifact, give each student an index card with certain data about the artifact provided, for example, depth, location, associations, and so forth.

☞ Have the students record their artifacts as accurately as possible using the Artifact Data Sheet.

☞ Compare results and discuss.

☞ Let the class judge which artifact sketch is the best.

Materials Needed:

artifacts or tools
poster board
Artifact Data Sheets
pens or pencils
index cards

Vocabulary:

artifact
ecofact
in situ

GETTING THE BIG PICTURE

Participants in archaeology tend to get a relatively confined view of what is going on. As students focus their interests on individual jobs, they naturally narrow their perspectives. Though moving individuals around into different jobs does mitigate against narrow focus to some extent, it still falls short of providing the optimum overview.

To bring the young archaeologists into a more complete understanding of what is happening sitewide, to update them on discoveries taking place apart from where they are, and to give them a sense of greater participation in the site's excavation, the teacher should hold periodic "big-picture" sessions. The purpose of the big-picture session is to discuss any new finds or any methodological turns the dig director wishes to take, giving students the opportunity to see the site from the teacher or dig director's perspective. Such sessions—held as often as warranted—go a long way toward teaching skills in synthesis while providing students with the knowledge they later need to make intelligent decisions, evaluations, and judgments about the site.

Classroom "chalk talks" are certainly valuable from time to time, but the greatest benefit comes from using the site itself as the chalkboard. Move around to different places on the site as the need arises and give everyone an opportunity to ask questions, comment, or take notes.

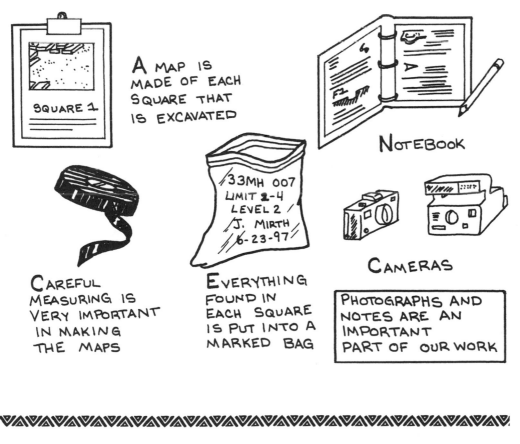

SQUARE 1

A MAP IS MADE OF EACH SQUARE THAT IS EXCAVATED

NOTEBOOK

33MH 007
UMIT 2-4
LEVEL 2
J. MIRTH
6-23-97

CAMERAS

CAREFUL MEASURING IS VERY IMPORTANT IN MAKING THE MAPS

EVERYTHING FOUND IN EACH SQUARE IS PUT INTO A MARKED BAG

PHOTOGRAPHS AND NOTES ARE AN IMPORTANT PART OF OUR WORK

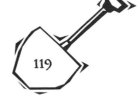

KEEPING A PHOTO RECORD

A picture is worth a thousand words—this adage is as true for archaeology as for anything else. Photographic control over the excavation is vital. Photos serve to link all of the recording systems and show, better than anything, the day-by-day progress from the time you encounter the site until the excavation ends. Keeping in mind that a successful result of every excavation is an empty hole in the ground, it behooves one to make as complete a photo record as possible.

Cameras serve a dual purpose on a dig. On one hand, they are valuable tools for recording data otherwise not removable from the site, such as stratigraphy, site overviews, unit features, walls, and so forth. Professional archaeologists generally use both black-and-white film and 35mm slides for this purpose. Apart from its use in recording necessary site information, the camera is also a handy and ideal tool for capturing the vitality, action, and real excitement of the dig. Taking pictures of the students working at their various jobs helps enhance the spirit of the endeavor.

Allowing each student a turn as official site photographer is a great idea, as it offers them not only the opportunity to enhance camera skills, but also to judge which features are important enough to warrant photography. In addition, the photographic aspect of the dig gives youngsters an introduction to the artistic side of archaeology. Teachers can use color slides taken at the site to reach a wider audience, and they can make the later showing of the slides—along with an accompanying commentary—an integral part of the archaeological lesson.

Equipment

The amount and types of photographic equipment you have depends, of course, on your resources. Basically, you should have at least two cameras available, one holding 35mm slides, the other holding black-and-white film. The teacher retains these cameras, which are for the photographs of record—the "official" site photographs.

The slide camera should be a 35mm single lens reflex camera with a built-in light meter, if possible. The single lens reflex avoids the problem of parallax, providing through-the-lens viewing with the same lens that takes the picture. The second camera can be of the same type, but uses black-and-white film instead. Why two kinds of film? The black-and-white photographs provide a daily record of the excavation, recording architectural features, artifacts, and other finds *in situ*, as well as panoramic site views. Black-and-white photographs are usually devoid of people and activity—purely "business" so to speak—and are taken for scientific rather than journalistic reasons. The slides, however, serve another purpose entirely. While they occasionally serve the same purpose as black-and-white photographs, slides are primarily taken for later presentation in illustrated lectures to interested groups. Slides may portray people and activities as well as the site material itself. Encouraging youngsters to bring along their own cameras (of whatever kind) will add to the dig's vitality and, at the same time, provide the students with a permanent record they can share with their classmates, parents, and friends.

Photographic Suggestions

The following suggestions should enhance the informative quality of the photographs you take as part of your formal archaeological record (as opposed to your general site photos or "people pictures").

- Make sure the subject shows sharp definition and contrast, leaving the viewer with an impression of clarity of detail.
- Sweep the subject to be photographed clean (no loose dirt, leaves, roots, footprints, etc.).
- Remove all intrusive objects from the picture, that is, tools, people, clothing, notebooks, and so forth.
- Place a directional arrow and unobtrusive scaling device (a trowel works nicely in both capacities) parallel to the side or bottom of the picture and oriented north.
- Make sure the subject being photographed completely fills the frame.
- Identify the unit, depth, and so forth, of the subject. Use a small chalkboard or menu board for this purpose, and place it in the lower corner of the photograph.
- Maintain a photo log and make an entry for each picture you take. This log becomes a permanent part of your archaeological record. (See Appendix B for a copy of a typical Photo Record Log.)

☞ Activities #29 & #30 ☜

KEEPING A PHOTO RECORD:
ACTIVITIES

ACTIVITY NO. 29

Activity: Watch the Birdie!

Subject: Art, Language Arts

Rationale: This activity will (1) demonstrate the rudiments of good picture-taking while (2) emphasizing the importance of site photography.

Objectives: Students will learn how to increase the informative quality of their photographs.

Activity Preparation:

☞ Show the class a 35mm camera and point out the *necessary* knobs and adjustments (don't get too technical) needed for clear picture-taking. Also show a simpler, automatic, "point-and-shoot" camera of the sort in common use today.

☞ Discuss the essence of good "informative" *photography.* Use a chalkboard or poster board to list the suggestions on good photography (i.e., the use of *directional arrows, scaling devices,* etc.).

☞ Show some slides of digs (available through mail order houses or from local museums, national or state historic parks, etc.—see Appendix A) and discuss various aspects of the archaeologists' success as recorders and conveyors of information.

Activity:

☞ Assign each student the job of bringing in three site "photographs." These "photos," taken from magazines or elsewhere, should be pictures of ruins or something that could be thought of as an archaeological site.

☞ Give each student three 4" x 6" index cards, some paste or rubber cement, and scissors, and instruct them to create "photographs" by pasting the pictures to the index cards and trimming them to fit. Have each student write the name of the site on the back of each card.

☞ Post the "photos" on the bulletin board for the entire class to see. Discuss which criteria should be met to make a good archaeological photo.

ACTIVITY NO. 29

Materials Needed: 35mm camera
automatic camera
slides
pictures of sites
4" x 6" index cards
paste or rubber cement
poster board
scissors

Vocabulary: photography
directional arrow
scaling device

ACTIVITY NO. 30

Activity:	Filling Out the Photo Log
Subjects:	Art, Language Arts
Rationale:	This activity will familiarize students with the importance of keeping accurate records.
Objectives:	The students will learn how to fill out a Photo Record Log.

Activity Preparation:

- ☞ Explain the need to keep an accurate *log* of your site photographs, especially when you are taking so many and detail is so important.
- ☞ Using a poster board replica of a Photo Record Log, point out the various columns and the importance of each. Discuss.

Activity:

- ☞ Have each student bring from home two or three photos of scenery or of people outdoors. Have the students put their names on the back of their photos.
- ☞ Give each student a copy of the Photo Record Log along with three of the "photographs" done earlier and pasted on the bulletin board.
- ☞ Have each student, using the six pictures, fill out the Photo Record Log.
- ☞ Compare results and discuss.

Materials Needed:
photographs
pictures (previously done by students)
pens or pencils
Photo Record Log

Vocabulary: log

126

CLEANING, LABELING, AND CATALOGING

Digging up and carefully recording the artifacts is important; washing, curating, and properly labeling and cataloging them is equally important. As discussed earlier, archaeologists bag artifacts in the field and label each bag. If an archaeologist fails to label the individual specimens according to their location in the site, their utility as tools to understanding the past is lost. Archaeologists should carefully mark each artifact in such a way that they can always specify its provenience. American professionals use a trinomial system (discussed earlier) that denotes the state, county, and site from which the artifact came. They also use a specific in-site location designator to record the position of the artifact within the dig. These designation codes will eventually appear on both the bag (done in the field) and the individual artifacts (done back in the classroom or laboratory). This double marking is necessary because the bags themselves will ultimately be tossed away (or stored), and the artifacts will be separated into various lots for different purposes.

The System

A cataloging system exists to provide an accurate and permanent means for determining the precise original location of each recorded artifact or specimen. As we are limited by the small size of many of our artifacts, we must, in some way, abbreviate or code our identification system. We must pack maximum information in a minimal space. The clearest way to explain the logic of the coding that finally appears on each artifact is to follow a typical artifact—let's say an old dinner fork—from its initial finding to its ultimate labeling.

First, the excavators put the fork into the unit bag, which they label with the site number, specific unit and level, date, and their own initials or names. They take the bag back to the classroom (lab) and assign a field specimen (FS) number to the entire bag *in the order of its processing.* The bag in which our fork sits receives the number "FS 31" (i.e., it is the 31st bag processed). The material from bag "FS 31" (including our fork) is then carefully removed, cleaned, and readied for labeling and cataloging. Our "FS 31" lot consists of 45 separate specimens. The fork is the fourth of these artifacts entered into the accession log. The *accession log* is the catalog which indexes all of the individual specimens recovered from the site. This catalog serves (1) to determine the full extent of the artifacts recovered; (2) to furnish a description of each artifact; and (3) to provide locational information on all specimens. Because our fork was the fourth item cataloged, it acquires the code, "FS 31-4." Of the thousands of artifacts we might recover from our site, only one—our fork—bears the signature "FS 31-4." Somewhere down the line if someone picks up the fork, he or she can go to the accession log, look up the number, and determine precisely where it came from! That's why proper labeling is so important.

☞ Activity #31 ☞

Cleaning the Artifact

Before artifacts can be properly labeled, studied, and displayed, they must be cleaned and, if necessary, repaired. Cleaning is generally a straightforward process involving dish soap, warm water, old toothbrushes, vegetable brushes (for scrubbing), and colanders (for drying). It doesn't hurt to have a bottle brush or two handy in case you uncover some narrow-necked bottles.

First, separate the artifacts into their different material categories, for example, glass, plastic, ceramic, wood, metal, bone, and so forth. Glass and ceramics are sturdy materials best cleaned with the brushes. Wet- or dry-scrub the other materials, depending how friable they are. *Good sense* is the key phrase here. Obviously you don't want to scrub your artifact into nothingness. Sometimes a dry toothbrush is a perfectly adequate cleaning tool. Let each artifact, depending on its material, fragility, or both, dictate its appropriate handling.

Repairing the Artifact

After you have satisfactorily cleaned and dried the artifacts, it is time to render first-aid to them, if needed. While the preservation techniques archaeologists use with real artifacts are very aggressive and entail a wide range of chemicals and sometimes

elaborate treatments, your major problem will probably involve the relatively simple repair of broken objects. Your principal remedy is normally nothing more complex than white glue, which is still the mainstay of the preservationist's "medicine chest." It has several major advantages: it is a sufficiently strong adhesive; it bonds most porous and semi-porous materials; it dries clear (thereby, not detracting from the repaired artifact itself); it is water-soluble (meaning you can remove it by soaking and, hence, re-do any bungled repair jobs); and it is relatively inexpensive. Its principal drawback, which will be of no relevance to your project, is that since it is an organic compound, its use would negate the possibility of radiocarbon dating any material on which it was used. You can repair non-porous materials like glass or metals with any of a number of epoxy resins readily available in hardware stores.

☞ Activity #32 ☞

Labeling the Artifact

Labeling the artifacts is the most time-consuming of the post-excavatory procedures but also one of the most critical. Here's what you need to do the job: indelible black India ink, a set of No. 102 crow quill pens (available from many stationers and bookstores), white correction fluid, and clear fingernail polish. All of the equipment is readily available and inexpensive, and it does a first-rate job.

Here are the steps to take in labeling your specimens.

1. Decide ahead of time just what information you are going to put on your artifact. *Remember—artifact size is a prime determinant.* Let's say we are going to put the site designation "33MH9" along with the FS number "FS 31-4" on our fork [**Note:** While the label "FS 31-4" does not indicate specifically where in the site the fork came from, it will lead any interested readers to the original location if they look in the accession log]. You can always streamline your designation to cut down its size; that is, eliminate "33MH" (since you obviously know where your site is and "9" is the only one you'll be dealing with), or drop the "FS" from "FS 31-4." This would leave you with "9-31-4" or, if you prefer, 31-4, and would be just fine for your purposes.

2. Label each artifact in a place where you can fit your designator code but, at the same time, *keep it from being too obvious.* In other words, "hide" the detracting label from plain view.

3. Print as *small* and as *clearly* as you can.

4. If you can write directly on the artifact or specimen without adding any additional material, do so using the crow quill pen and your black India ink.

5. If your surface is too porous, lumpy, corroded, or the wrong color and does not allow just the use of ink, then apply a *thin* coat of correction fluid in the place you want the label to go. Let dry a minute or so. [**Note:** It saves a lot of time to

run this step on several specimens at once. And keep the lids on the correction fluid bottles when not in use—the fluid dries out very quickly!]

6.   Atop the white patch created by your correction fluid, print your code with crow quill and black ink. (Be careful not to scratch too deeply into your patch).

7.   Finally, cover each label—those laid directly on the artifact surface as well as those put down on the white patches—with a coating of clear fingernail polish. This coating, when it dries, serves to make the label permanent.

8.   If the artifacts are too small to be individually labeled (i.e., a bunch of loose beads), put them together in a small, clear vial or plastic container, and label it.

Once you clearly label your artifacts, they are free of the confines of the bag you put them in, and you can handle, study, and display them in any manner you wish.

☞ Activity #33 ☜

Ironclad Rule #7—The main thing in cataloging is to ensure that you keep an accurate record of where each item came from. The actual labeling system you employ to achieve this is up to you (and your imaginative students).

CLEANING, LABELING, AND CATALOGING:
ACTIVITIES AND WORK SHEETS

ACTIVITY NO. 31

Activity: The Accession Log

Subjects: Science, Social Studies

Rationale: This activity will help acquaint students with the way archaeologists keep track of artifacts and specimens once they are out of the field.

Objectives: The students will learn how to give artifacts their proper field specimen numbers and enter these numbers into the accession log.

Activity Preparation:

☞ Explain how artifacts and specimens are handled once the bag they are in gets back to the laboratory/classroom. Go through the process step-by-step, answering questions as you go.

☞ Using a prepared, labeled bag with three or four items in it, demonstrate how the entire bag gets its field specimen number, or *FS number*. Then, show how all of the *individual items* in the bag get their own subdesignations.

☞ Using the chalkboard or a poster board replica of an accession log page, list your artifacts, explaining your logic as you go.

☞ Show how the final label that each specimen receives is unique.

Activity:

☞ Give each student a paper lunch bag. The teacher can give the bags a "unit" label ahead of time or they can have the students label their own—something they learned to do in an earlier activity/exercise.

☞ Instruct the students to bring the bags to class with *three* small items in them. Pre-label the artifacts from one through three.

☞ Have the students, one at a time, come with their bags to a central location where the teacher, while explaining, marks an FS number on each bag.

☞ Hand out accession log sheets and have the students enter their respective artifacts.

Materials Needed: artifacts   poster board
paper lunch bags   pens or pencils
accession log sheets

Vocabulary: accession number   FS number

ACTIVITY NO. 32

Activity:	Pot Repair
Subjects:	Social Studies
Rationale:	This activity will acquaint students with the process of artifact repair.
Objectives:	The students will repair a broken ceramic vessel.

Activity Preparation:

☞ Explain how laboratory *preservational* techniques are an important tool to the archaeologist and to the *museologist*. Show pictures of archaeological remains in various stages of disrepair and discuss with the class what might be done to repair them.

☞ Demonstrate how to repair a pot by putting together *shards* of a previously broken *ceramic* item. Show how to position the vessel and nestle it in the sand so that the glue has the opportunity to dry.

☞ Get a ceramic vessel or other item for *each student* in the class—cups, ashtrays, saucers, flower pots, knick-knacks, and figurines are all suitable—and carefully break them into several pieces. [**Note:** Because of the potential mess, you will likely want to do this breaking in a home work area.]

☞ Put the pieces of each broken vessel in a separate plastic bag, one for each student. [**Note:** Leave a piece or two missing from each set so as to imitate more accurately the realities of an archaeological find.]

Activity:

☞ Divide the class into "museum teams" and provide each team with a shallow box or basin of sand and two bottles of white glue.

☞ Give each student a bag of ceramic fragments with the instructions that they are to repair the pieces as skillfully as they can.

☞ When completed (and it will take several days due to the glue's drying time), have the students line up their finished products as in a museum display.

Materials Needed:

pictures of archaeological remains	ceramics
sand containers	white glue
plastic bags	

Vocabulary:

preservation	museologist
ceramics	shards

133

▽△▽△▽△▽△▽△▽△▽△▽△▽△▽△▽△▽△▽△▽△▽△▽△▽△▽△

ACTIVITY NO. 33

▽△▽△▽△▽△▽△▽△▽△▽△▽△▽△▽△▽△▽△▽△▽△▽△▽△▽△

Activity: Labeling Artifacts

Subjects: Social Studies, Art, Language Arts

Rationale: This exercise will acquaint the students with the reasons for and the processes involved in artifact labeling.

Objectives: The students will learn how to label an artifact correctly.

Activity Preparation:

☞   Explain to the students that once the artifacts are separated from their bags they must be given a *permanent* label. Discuss the variety of ways to present the label.

☞   Along with the class, decide on an identification label that works best for you. *Remember,* it has to contain certain minimal information.

☞   Demonstrate to the class, using a few different artifactual materials, just how to label an artifact. Go through all of the steps from correction fluid to clear fingernail polish. Explain how correction fluid is used *only when necessary.* Show the need to write small, clearly, and in an *inconspicuous* spot.

Activity:

☞   Have each student bring three or four "artifacts" from home. Make sure they are items that have been discarded. Tell the students to make them small and of different materials.

☞   Divide the class into teams and give each team crow quill pens (one for each student), a bottle of black India ink, a bottle of white correction fluid, and a bottle of clear fingernail polish.

☞   Instruct each student to label the artifacts they brought from home as shown.

☞   Hold a contest to see which student can print a label the smallest and the clearest.

Materials Needed: artifacts   crow quill pens (No. 102)
                               black India ink   correction fluid
                               clear fingernail polish

Vocabulary: permanent   inconspicuous

MAINTAIN A REPOSITORY

When excavating any site—even a seemingly empty lot—archaeologists are often surprised at the great number and variety of objects they find. They separate these artifacts and specimens into categories for later analysis, comparison, and description. This compartmentalization requires space; for this reason, a portion of the classroom has to be set aside for the establishment of a repository.

The most desirable repository places the artifacts in plain view at all times, readily accessible to both sight and study. This keeps the idea of them in the front of students' minds and serves to spur their creative instincts. Also, the artifact visibility allows the students to show off the fruits of their efforts proudly to classroom visitors. If space availability prohibits full-time display of the artifacts, store them in strong cartons, plainly marked as to content, and readily available for artifact retrieval. Plastic resealable freezer bags (which come in a variety of sizes) are a great way to store your artifacts. They are strong, capacious, clear, and easy to secure.

Segregating the Artifacts

Once you have properly labeled the artifacts and specimens, their provenience is a permanent part of them, and you may move them about freely without worry of "misfiling" them. You must decide how you will store your artifacts. You can do this by industry or material, by location or unit in the site, or by function. Each way has its advantages, and individual needs will dictate what's best in each case.

To the archaeologist, the word *industry* applies to all of those artifacts from a site made from the same material. Segregating by industry is one way to handle your artifact inventory. Archaeological site reports, especially prehistoric ones, commonly contain chapter headings like *Ceramics, Lithics* (stone), or *Bone,* each discussing the artifacts by class and type. Then, if you are comparing items made from the same material—as would be the case, for instance, if you were trying to determine the range of colors represented in your recovered glass artifacts—having similar material all in one place would be very convenient for efficient examination.

Another means of storing your artifacts is by their location within the site. Keeping the batches of artifacts together regardless of material, but based only on the dig units they came from, allows the young archaeologist to begin to determine *activity loci,* or the ways in which different parts of the site were utilized. Such activity area determinations are a primary goal of most archaeological study.

Historical archaeologists particularly (and your site will *always* fit this category) prefer to utilize a system that segregates artifacts by the functions they served. You might, for example, separate artifacts as *Personal Items* (things directly associated with personal use such as jewelry, tobacco pipes, or harmonicas); *Domestic Items* (dinnerware, utensils, furniture parts, etc.); *Architectural* or *Building Materials* (nails, screws, locks, etc.); *Transportation Items* (car parts, wagon parts, etc.); and so on down the line. You can be as specific as you wish. Many historical archaeologists prefer this means of separating artifacts because it provides a quick reference both to the kind of site they excavated and to the spectrum of activities that took place there.

The Rudiments

There are probably other ways to segregate your site specimens for further study, but *industry, association,* and *functional category* are the most likely choices. They have been time-tested. However you choose to sort your artifacts, you will want to take note of certain rudiments.

- Clean and label all artifacts and specimens before putting them into the repository.
- Whatever system you decide upon, every individual involved in the project should be acquainted with it so as to reduce confusion and the misfiling of materials. Make sure the word gets out and is understood.
- Store all of the parts of the same artifact together in the same container, unless you elected to compartmentalize by in-site association.
- Whenever possible, utilize clear containers. Polyethylene envelopes are optimum (and expensive!), but clear plastic bags are more than adequate. Keep several packages of various sizes on hand. Also, clear plastic pill containers with snaplids are extremely useful. Most local pharmacists will gladly contribute several of these to an educational project like yours.
- Consolidate your collection. If you have your archaeological specimens scattered all over the classroom, you stand a much better chance of losing track of, or

worse, just plain losing your specimens. *Remember: a repository is not a museum. Its principal purpose is to store systematically, not to display.*

- Arrange your repository so that the most important specimens, at least, are easily accessible and in plain view. Students need to be reminded visually of what they are working with. Unfortunately, something out of sight too often becomes something out of mind.

Selecting Your Storage Mode

Allowing the students—with the teacher's guidance, of course, and after detailed discussion of the pros and cons of each—to choose the storage mode they wish to work with may well have a pedagogic value. Not only does giving them such a choice enhance their sense of participation, but it also serves as an excellent assessment tool for evaluating student progress. This is because to make a valid judgment, the student must understand what has been going on up to this point.

☞ Activity #34 ☞

Building (Physically) Your Repository

First you need to set aside a space in your classroom for the repository. Next, you must pull together your materials and build storage facilities, using cartons, tables, trays, boxes, and so forth. The actual "architecture" of your repository can become a part of the lesson. The youngsters will love it!

☞ Activity #35 ☞

Any kind of repository will make at least some spatial demands on your classroom. The amount of space necessary depends entirely on your own needs and instructional goals (always keeping in mind, of course, that archaeology is a *cumulative* science whose collection of specimens continuously grows). Some teachers may want to contain the material very tightly, while others may wish to make it a centerpiece of their classroom. Either way, you will want to have certain things as part of your storage unit.

An adequate and easily accessible storage system is a necessity. Low cost isn't a bad trait either. You do not want your artifacts and specimens scattered in various locations around the room. They are too easily lost, strayed, or (perish the thought!) stolen. On the other hand, you should be able to get in and out of the storage facility with a minimum of fuss. Plastic milk crates are excellent building blocks for your

storage structure. They are relatively cheap, long-lasting, tough (i.e. child-proof), colorful (you could even color code your material with them), stackable, interlocking, and easily portable. Few things are more accommodating for your uses.

Cigar boxes make excellent storage units for smaller artifacts, principally because of their solidity and strength (I've had some in continuous use for 25 years). They close tightly and can be neatly stacked. A taped-on index card listing their contents makes them an ideal repository container. These are readily available from your local tobacconist or smoke-shop owner.

For open display of items, either during storage or during study, Styrofoam, heavy paper, or cardboard meat or vegetable trays (like the ones in your supermarket) are great for table-top use. You may be able to talk your local butcher or produce manager into donating a hundred or so (I can't imagine you needing more) or even selling them to you at cost, which is around two or three cents each.

Small plastic pill containers or plastic bags work well for storing buttons and coins. Besides the advantage of having a tight seal, pill containers and plastic bags are transparent, allowing one to see their contents before opening them. They provide protection, consolidation, and visibility all at the same time.

If your site turns out to have some genuinely exciting specimens that you might want to have on public display for visitors in your classroom, in the library, in the principal's office, or in a hallway display case, then you might give some thought to purchasing a couple of Riker (or similar) specimen mounts. These well-made professional display trays consist of a sturdy cardboard container packed solidly from top to bottom with absorbent cotton and covered with a glass lid. These mounts range in size (and, of course, price) from 2½"-by-3" (at about $3.50 each) up to 14"-by-21" (at about $20 each). If you are interested, write to Carolina Biological Supply Company at their main office on 2700 York Road, Burlington, NC 27215, or the Powell Laboratories Division, 19355 McLoughlin Blvd., Gladstone, OR 97027, whichever is more convenient, and ask for a free catalog. They are not cheap, to be sure, but they are top-of-the-line.

The Curation Table

Every repository requires a table or station at which the lab technician (student) or archaeologist can work, analyze, study, and carry out general curational chores on their artifacts and specimens. Having such a station puts the individual right in the middle of the collection and minimizes the transportation of specimens—and, of course, the opportunity to lose items. If you have adequate space, you may want more than one table. You can use the first table for analysis and artifact work and the second (or third?) to lay out your artifacts. Each teacher will have to decide which setup they can support logistically and spatially. But again, at least one table (the longer, the better) is required.

Your lab table should be outfitted properly for the work it is designed to perform. You'll want to have: a plastic basin with sand (for repairing artifacts), white glue, labeling supplies (including India ink, crow quills, correction fluid, and clear fingernail polish), ruler or scale (a linear calipers would be even better), graph paper, index cards, a magnifying glass, and a note pad. Leave room for two or three chairs so that more than one student can use the repository station simultaneously.

In the end, your repository will be an area of high activity in your classroom. Regularly supplied with newly recovered specimens from your site in need of treatment, it will be in constant use. Make it as efficient and as pedagogically valuable as you can.

☞ Activity #36 ☞

MAINTAIN A REPOSITORY:
ACTIVITIES, WORK SHEETS, AND EXTENSIONS

ACTIVITY NO. 34

Activity:	Separating the Artifacts
Subjects:	Social Studies, Science
Rationale:	This exercise will help students to understand the importance of an orderly repository to an archaeologist.
Objectives:	The students will know how to separate artifacts by functional category.

Activity Preparation:

☞ Discuss what happens to specimens once they are back in the laboratory (classroom). Explain how to use a *repository* for storage and as a place to work on and study artifacts and specimens. If possible, arrange a visit to the repository of a local *museum* or university.

☞ Explain the concept of *industry*, all of the artifacts made of one kind of material found at a single site, and discuss how historical artifacts are more difficult to categorize by industry because of the wide range of modern materials. Use a wide array of modern artifacts to demonstrate this complexity.

☞ Explain functional categories. Using the same array of artifacts, separate them into groups by similarity of use or function, that is, toys, personal items, kitchen items, auto parts, and so forth. Elicit discussion on related issues.

☞ Prepare some index cards with a functional category written on each.

Activity:

☞ Direct each student to bring an artifact from home.

☞ Display the brought-in artifacts on a center table and, one-at-a-time, have the class decide which industry they belong with. Separate them physically and discuss "gray" areas.

☞ Spread out the pre-marked index cards and have the class rearrange the artifacts under each according to function.

☞ Have each of the students fill out a Functional Categories Work Sheet. Compare results and discuss.

Materials Needed:

artifacts	index cards
pens or pencils	work sheets

Vocabulary:

repository	museum
industry	function

ARTIFACT FUNCTIONS WORK SHEET

We have learned that we can separate our artifacts for storage or discussion in one of several ways. One common method is to separate them by the material from which they are made, or industry; another is to separate them by their general function or use. Organizing artifacts by their functions or uses is popular among archaeologists who deal with historical sites.

Let's see what you would do with these historic or modern artifacts!

Instructions

Common artifacts that might be found at a site are listed in the left-hand column below. Study each one carefully, and then match it with a functional category from the right-hand column.

ARTIFACTS

1. shirt _____
2. fork _____
3. dust pan _____
4. leash _____
5. nail _____
6. tobacco pipe _____
7. rosary _____
8. safety pin _____
9. bullet _____
10. dime _____
11. hatchet _____
12. horseshoe _____
13. soda bottle _____
14. candle _____
15. screwdriver _____
16. rabbit's foot _____
17. key _____
18. clock _____
19. brick _____
20. yo-yo _____

CATEGORIES

A. Personal Items

B. Domestic or Household Items

C. Building Materials

D. Transportation Items

E. Tools

F. Commerce Items

THE FUNCTIONAL CLASSIFICATION OF ARTIFACTS

A. **Personal Items**—Things directly associated with individual, personal use
   Examples:
   clothing   footwear
   jewelry   toys
   indulgences (pipes, cigars, etc.)
   personal effects

B. **Domestic or Household Items**—Things associated with the house or home, in general
   Examples:
   houseware   appliances
   furniture   decorations (pictures, etc.)
   kitchenware   utensils
   cleaning equipment

C. **Building Materials**—Things that make up the physical parts of the building structure itself
   Examples:
   nails   bricks
   electrical parts   water pipes
   window panes

D. **Tools**—All items commonly referred to as tools in the normal sense of the word
   Examples:
   hammers   axes
   drills   saws

E. **Transportation Items**—Things associated with all manners of transportation
   Examples:
   automobile parts   carriage parts
   bike parts   horseshoes

F. **Commercial Items**—Items commonly associated with the world of business or commerce
   Examples:
   machine parts   office equipment

ACTIVITY NO. 35

Activity:	Building a Repository
Subjects:	Social Studies, Art, Language Arts
Rationale:	This activity will acquaint the students with (1) the needs of a repository; and (2) the jobs carried out there.
Objectives:	The students will learn (1) what kinds of things are necessary for properly equipping a classroom repository; and (2) what kinds of activities take place there.

Activity Preparation:

☞ Review with the class the functions of a repository, which is a place where archaeological specimens go for treatment and storage prior to museum display.

☞ Share your ideas of the proposed classroom repository and call for suggestions. Make a point of telling the students what the basic requirements are. Make a list on the chalkboard of the kinds of containers and storage units you will need and where they might be obtained.

Activity:

☞ Divide the class into "construction gangs" and assign different tasks to each gang.

☞ Assign some students the job of rounding up the boxes, containers, and so forth, for the repository.

☞ Assign other students the task of actually building and labeling the station.

☞ Make sure that all opinions are heard and considered.

Materials Needed:

various containers/units for storage	magnifying glass
clear fingernail polish	"zippered" plastic sandwich bags
plastic basin	sand
correction fluid	black India ink
crow quill pens (No. 102)	white glue
index cards	ruler or measuring tape

ACTIVITY NO. 36

Activity:	Ribbon-Cutting!
Subjects:	Art, Language Arts
Rationale:	This activity will offer the students the opportunity to (1) appreciate the efforts that they put into the construction of their repository; and (2) reward themselves for the work done.
Objectives:	The students will conduct an "official" ribbon-cutting ceremony in recognition of their efforts.

Activity Preparation:

☞ Explain to the class how societies often celebrate when they successfully complete a project. Explain how the *celebration* recognizes the efforts of the builders (the students) and the people who support them (the parents, teachers, administrators, and merchants).

☞ Detail what kinds of activities are a part of such a *ceremony.*

☞ Offer your services as a *consultant,* but allow the students to manage the affair as much as possible.

Activity:

☞ Elect a small group (two or three) to serve as a steering committee for the event. Have *them* do the following:

- Make some students responsible for bringing cookies and other refreshments from home.
- Have some students decorate the room, set up the ribbon, and prepare the ceremonial scissors.
- Have some students prepare short "addresses" to give at the ceremony.
- Have some students prepare and send written invitations to the principal and other "luminaries" (Don't forget those tradespeople who gave you equipment, boxes, etc.).*
- Conduct an "official" ribbon-cutting ceremony with the actual cutting and the speeches.
- Serve refreshments.

*Note: You might even consider inviting the local press and TV station.

ACTIVITY NO. 36

Materials Needed: refreshments (with cups, plates, etc.)
decorations (including the ribbon)
scissors (decorated)
podium (for the speeches)

Vocabulary: celebration
ceremony
consultant

PRODUCE A SITE REPORT

An old saying among archaeologists attributed to the pioneer 19th-century archaeologist, Augustus Pitt-Rivers, holds that a discovery dates only from the time of its recording, and not from the time of its actual discovery in the soil. How true!

Field archaeology is essentially destructive; once a site is dug it cannot be dug again. A hard and fast rule of archaeology states that archaeologists must report promptly on *all* sites they dig. Since all of the recovered evidence initially remains solely in the minds, memories, and notes of the diggers themselves, archaeologists must write site reports to put the evidence into a form useful for other interested persons. *And so must you.*

Have an archaeologist provide you with a real site report to serve as a model. Most of them have ample spare copies that they would be glad to see put to good use. Collect a number of them and make them readily available to your students. You will immediately see that such reports contain several modes of presentation, including graphs, charts, tables, drawings, maps, photographs, and, of course, text. Chapter headings show the wide range of topics covered. Assign students or teams of students to the various tasks, and have them work toward a cohesive and comprehensive presentation of their work. Putting together and editing this monograph will give the students experience in multiple academic skills. Perhaps as important as anything else, they will have produced, by and for themselves, a lasting memorial to their hard work and scholastic achievement. The availability of desktop publishing software makes production of a professional-looking report a real possibility. The teacher can add to this tribute by giving the school library its own copy or distributing copies to friends in other schools.

What should go into the site report? After examining a dozen professionally written archaeological site reports, one would find a certain consistency of reportage. A few sections or chapter headings might appear in a different order or wording from one report to the next, but you are likely to find that all of the parts are there in much the same sequence of discussion. Of course, you're not a professional archaeologist, and you're not writing to an audience of archaeologists or other scientists. You are a teacher, and your purpose in undertaking this relatively complex archaeological project, while manifold, is primarily to turn your youngsters on to the whole, wide, wonderful world of ideas and learning. Therefore, you must modify the site report to suit *your* needs—no one else's. However, since up to now you have been so diligent in "following the rules" of good, sound methodology, why stop? The report is the intellectual capstone of your students' efforts (as well as your own).

It is likely that your youngsters will be working at different grade and skill levels. In addition, your dig will probably not be completed in one class unit, so rather than thinking of a *final* report, think in terms of an *interim* report or a *works-in-progress.* Whatever the case, the teacher can look at the range of site reports, determine what sections are within the capabilities of their students, and tailor the assignment accordingly. You as teacher may want to use a series of poster boards representing pages and report sections and containing both the kind of information desired and an example of it. Although the level of writing and data exposition will differ between classes, your students should all be able to understand what the report requires. It's not whether they know the complete answer (after all, who does?), rather that they understand the question.

> Ironclad Rule Number #8—Any site, even your "empty lot,"
> without a final report is a no-no!

Set Up an Editorial Board

It's probably a good idea to establish a board of "editors" responsible for different aspects of the report. Of course, you could rotate these positions among the students, giving each one the opportunity to control some level of decision-making. Editorial "heads" might supervise photography, artwork, design and layout, proofing, and so forth. An editor-in-chief could serve to tie the whole report together.

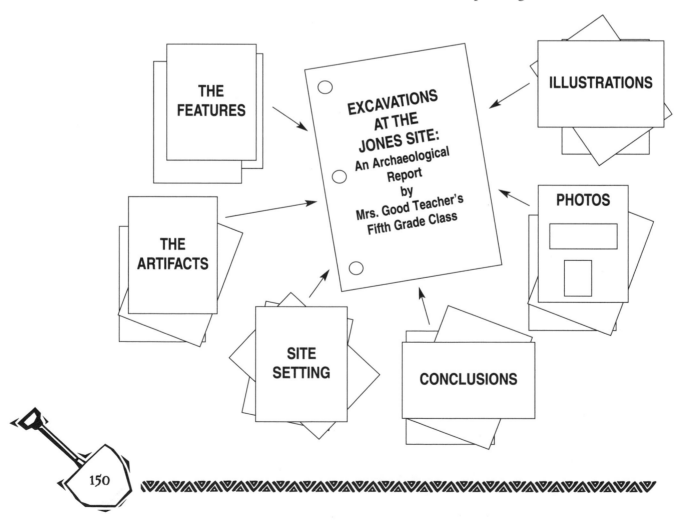

☞ Activity #37 ☜

Content of the Typical Site Report

The following is a model for your site report. Adjust it to your particular needs and class level. Each set of brackets (> <) indicates a report section, which is followed by an explanation of its content.

In addition, each section contains an example of the kind of description and presentation that takes place there. Youngsters can handle it—don't underestimate them (especially with your guidance)!

>Title Page<

On this sheet, put the title of your report, and list the authors of the various sections and their affiliations (school, grade, etc.).
Example: "The Archaeological Excavation of the Jones Site (33MH007)"
by
[The class names would go here].

>Abstract<

A short statement—fewer than 200 words—which is a synopsis or summary of your objectives, findings, and so forth.
Example: "The excavation of the Jones site led to the recovery of 2,300 artifacts, 118 bone specimens, and 24 features. After careful examination, we determine that the site was at one time a small grocery store. …"

>Table of Contents<

List the topics discussed along with the pages on which they appear.
Example:

Abstract	1
Acknowledgments	2
Introduction	3
Environmental Description	4

>Acknowledgments<

Acknowledgments serve as a statement of appreciation to anyone who has been of special help in your archaeological work (e.g., the landowner who let you dig, your principal, teacher, parents, etc.).
Example: "The class wishes to thank Miss Goodteacher for her help in carrying

out this archaeological project. Thanks also to Principal Smith for …" [Thank all of the people who helped make this project a success and tell how they helped.]

>Introduction<

Briefly tell the reader the nature of your project, the site name, the reason for its name, its location, what you did at the site, how many people worked on it, how long the work took, and so forth. Include one or two maps here, one locating the site in the state, and the other a close-up showing the site in reference to nearby landmarks.

Example: "We undertook the excavation of this site in order to better understand what happened there historically. Located in Mahoning County, OH, the Jones site took its name from the present owner of the property who gave us kind permission to excavate. The fifth grade class of 23 members worked on this site from [Dates] and took 21 weeks to complete the work. …" [A location map (or two) should be included in this section.]

>Environmental Setting<

Discuss the geology and soils in the site area, as well as the site's relationship to nearby physiographic features such as mountains, rivers, streams, lakes, valleys, and so forth. Discuss any native flora (plants) and fauna (animals).

Example: "The Jones site sits on a low terrace adjacent to the Mahoning River. The area immediately surrounding it is now commercially developed, but wooded areas are nearby. …" [Describe the environment in detail.]

>Preliminary Research<

Provide a brief overview of what was known about the site before you excavated it. Discuss the fruits of your pre-excavatory library research and local informant interviews. If you have any copies of old photographs of your site's building before it was razed, include them here. Graphics may be important here.

Example: "Very little was known about the site before we excavated it. Several people who have lived in the area [Names] provided valuable information about its use. An examination of the City Directory informed us that …"

>Aims and Goals<

Explain the purpose of the project. What were you looking for? Why? Why this site and not another? *List your working hypotheses here.*

Example: "Initially we took on this project to acquaint students with the discipline of archaeology and how it works and to determine the functions the excavated site may have served. Our working hypotheses were [List them] …"

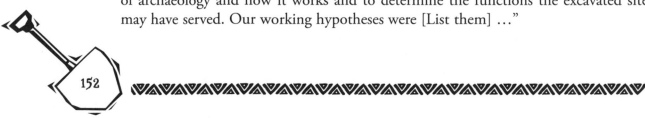

>Site Description<

Describe the site in some detail including dimensions, depth, elevation and surface features. Here you would include a carefully drawn site map showing the grid, units excavated, and so forth. Graphics are a necessity here.

Example: "The site measures 43 meters by 24 meters in size. A small section of brick wall, six meters long and two meters high, is still visible on the northern perimeter of the site. Broken bricks are scattered all over …"

>Field Methods<

Describe the actual *field* techniques employed at the site including unit size, depth units, tools used, and so forth.

Example: "We used a standard two-meter grid oriented north-south to divide the site into excavation units two-by-two meters in size. All soils were sifted through a quarter-inch screen. …" [Describe the actual details of what you did.]

>Laboratory Methods<

Describe your cataloging methods and any different or unusual procedures you might have used in handling your artifacts.

Example: "Once in the laboratory, all of the artifacts passed through the same routine. We washed, repaired, and separated them [Tell how] …"

>Main Body<

Discuss your findings in depth here. For optimum organization of your information, address specific finds under a variety of subheadings as follows:

>Stratigraphy<

Describe the stratigraphy. How many strata were present? What time spans did they represent? Include here any stratigraphic profiles you have drawn. Graphics *may* be called for here.

Example: "Three definitive strata or levels occur in the Jones site. The earliest strata (Layer 3), recognizable by the dark brown sandy soil surrounding it, represents the period from 1900 to 1925. Layer 2 was …" [A cross-section or profile drawing is called for here.]

>Features<

Describe all of your site features. Talk about each one in turn and fully discuss its dimensions, locations in the site, depth, functions or uses, likely associations with

other features, and so forth. Include photos, drawings, or both, of each of the various features here.

Example: "Feature 1—Feature 1 is a large brick wall, six meters long and two meters high, found on the northern perimeter of the site. [Make a detailed description of the feature (with complete measurements) and include a detailed drawing, photograph, or both.]

"Feature 2—Feature 2 is …"

>Artifacts<

Briefly summarize the recovered materials and, if there are multiple specimens in a category, include a summary table.

Example: "We found a total of 2,300 artifacts. Of this number, 1,400 were metal, 350 were ceramic, and the remainder were composed of multiple materials. A complete description of the artifacts by functional category follows.

>Household Artifacts<

Kitchenware: These are items usually associated with use in the kitchen or in food preparation. …" [Separate the artifacts into categories (functional categories are preferable for historic artifacts) and discuss in detail. The detailed description of all of your artifacts usually makes this the longest section in the report.]

>Faunal Remains<

Do the same thing here that you did with your artifactual specimens. Describe the various bones as to genus and species, location, depth, and so forth.

Example: "We recovered 118 bone specimens—75 from cattle, 25 from pigs, and 18 from chickens." [Describe in as much detail as you can.]

>Artifact and Feature Distribution<

Discuss here associations between artifacts and features and what these relationships mean. Tables are very useful in this section.

Example: "Our discovery of most of the kitchenware in the southeast corner of the site probably indicates that food preparation took place there. …"

>Chronology<

What do your artifacts and features say, if anything, about the site's age?

Example: "The artifacts indicate that the earliest activity at the site took place in 1900. The … are evidence of this. In 1920 …" [Let the dated artifacts dictate what happened when.]

>Summary and Conclusions<

First, summarize in a few paragraphs your work and findings at the site. Next, draw any conclusions you think suitable. This is a good time to restate your working hypotheses and use your findings to support or invalidate them.

Example: "The 2,300 artifacts, 118 bones, and 24 features that we recovered represent …" [Here you summarize (not detail, but summarize) your findings and draw conclusions about the site. **Note:** In professional reports, many archaeologists read this section first and from it decide if they need to read the remainder.]

>References (or Bibliography)<

Here you will list, in alphabetical order, all written sources that you used in researching and writing your site report.

Example: "Abbot, B. (1984). *Bones for the young archaeologist.* Waco, TX: Good Digging Press."

>Appendices<

Here include any ancillary studies done by individuals about various aspects of your site. For example, if one of your students does an in-depth study of a particular artifact or set of artifacts discovered, or maybe a detailed interview with a former site inhabitant, you can put the pieces here as separate studies.

PRODUCE A SITE REPORT:
ACTIVITIES

ACTIVITY NO. 37

Activity:	Setting Up a Site Report
Subjects:	Science, Social Studies, Geology, Geography, Art, Language Arts
Rationale:	This exercise will serve to acquaint students with (1) the various parts of a site report; and (2) the skills involved in producing such a report.
Objectives:	The students will know the necessary parts of an archaeological report.

Activity Preparation:

☞ Discuss the importance of completing a final (or *interim*) report of the archaeological project. Pass around or show several copies of professional reports, reading the table of contents to demonstrate similarities.

☞ Explain the need for certain individuals to handle editorial tasks, including writing, proofreading, and *graphic* design. Outline the duties of the various *editors*. Use a poster board flow chart to show the various relationships of the parts.

☞ Talk about the dig and the findings. Elicit questions and discussion.

☞ Go over the site report contents in detail.

☞ Describe the role of a *consultant* and how you will serve in that role.

Activity:

☞ Have the class hold elections to choose an editor.

☞ Allow the editor to choose the various department heads.

☞ Hand out the Archaeological Report Topic Outline (modify if necessary).

☞ Have the various department or section heads write about or illustrate (if they are involved in graphics) their respective subjects.

☞ Hold regular editorial meetings to see how the report is progressing.

☞ As consultant, keep the work moving in the right direction.

Materials Needed: site reports   Archaeology Report Topic Outlines
                     poster board

Vocabulary: interim
               editors
               consultant
               graphics

THE ARCHAEOLOGICAL REPORT
TOPIC OUTLINE

Editorial Section
> Title Page
> Abstract
> Table of Contents
> Acknowledgments

Introductory Section
> Introduction
> Environmental Setting
> Preliminary Research
> Aims and Goals
> Site Description
> Methodology
> Field Methods
> Laboratory Methods

Main Body
> Stratigraphy
> Features
> Artifacts
> Faunal Remains
> Artifact and Feature Distribution
> Chronology
> Summary and Conclusions

References

Appendices

CREATE A MUSEUM DISPLAY

With all the fieldwork done and the digging tools set aside for the season, you can present your artifactual treasures to the rest of the world. Setting up exhibits that draw the viewer's interest and effectively represent the work done and the information gathered is part of the discipline called museology. A proper exhibit highlights all aspects of the dig, with a special focus on some of the more interesting things found. The trick is to show the items recovered in such a way that they draw the observer into the site itself. A good museum display doesn't just have artifacts set out on a table with cardboard tags telling what they are, but exhibits them in a manner that maximizes their impact and keeps the audience in awe.

Creating a museum display will allow your young artists to contribute colorful backdrops or dioramas for the artifacts, while the creative writers of the class can compose description panels. Perhaps the school library can display the presentation in its glass cases, or maybe the principal will allow it to be displayed in the school foyer where a much wider audience can appreciate it.

Field Trips

A field trip to a local museum would be ideal at this point in your project. If you have a museum that you can visit, call ahead and try to arrange a behind-the-scenes tour. This will give your young archaeologists the opportunity to see the work that goes into making the effective out-front exhibits that the public loves.

Dioramas

Creating colorful and informative dioramas can add the dimension of aesthetics to your science course. Instead of merely placing your finds on a glass shelf, put them into a setting that makes them exciting as well as educational. Designing and rendering the backdrops can be a wonderful way for the artistically creative student to make a major contribution to a scientific end-product.

Dioramas should not be boring. You can do various kinds of illustrative, imaginative, and colorful backdrops for your artifacts and specimens. You can make a diorama depicting your site and its surroundings—perhaps a modern diorama showing your site surrounded by buildings, or maybe one showing what your lot might have looked like when it was inhabited.

☞ Activity #38 ☜

Be Imaginative!

One of the most innovative—yet simple—hallway museum exhibits that I have ever seen attracted viewers by the droves. And it accomplished this without a single artifact in sight! How? The imaginative young museologist (a high school student) who set it up relied on one of the strongest of human drives—curiosity—for his success. After carefully setting up his backdrops and dioramas in the hallway cabinets and glass display cases, he set about covering the glass almost entirely with construction paper, rendering everything inside the cases invisible to the eye of the casual observer. The key words here are *casual observer*. For a while ordinary passers-by would see nothing but colorful, paper-covered cases, "cryptic" messages like "Look here" or "The First Find" would tempt more curious observers to press their eyes against peepholes cut at strategic locations in the paper covering. As a reward for their curiosity, they saw a wonderfully imaginative arrangement of artifacts and information cards. The museologist's goal here was to draw attention to his exhibit by *not* making it so obvious. At the same time, by adding peepholes that took at least a modicum of effort to examine, he made the exhibit participatory.

Interpretive Exhibits

However, don't just put your artifacts out in a "finished setting"; interpret them for the viewer. The public has as much (in my experience, more) interest in what your young archaeologists *did* as in what they discovered. Observers may not be as interested in a broken soda bottle from the 1950s as they would be in knowing how your young curators put the whole thing back together again. So show them: put up an exhibit with a diorama, props, and so forth, showing a bottle in your sandbox being patiently put together with white glue. Such an exhibit interprets not only the bottle itself but also demonstrates the process of repairing it.

Because, by now, your site has probably been "put away"—at least for a year—the exhibit represents your site for those who never had the opportunity to see the real thing. Use the exhibit as a model of your site—show all of the strings laid out; have some of the units excavated, some not; show the table screens in place with your back-dirt piles. Have plenty of information cards telling what everything is. Let the non-participants in your archaeological adventure see as much as they can. If you make it plain to the students what it is you want to show, they will fly to the rescue! Your role as teacher in this area of the project will primarily involve holding on to the reins of youthful enthusiasm.

Having stood by countless tables laden with what most would have called prosaic artifacts, I have *never* failed to marvel at the excitement reflected in the eyes of the parents whose children had uncovered them. Soda bottles were elevated to the level of Ming Dynasty vases, and broken umbrella shafts became scepters of Zeus. Your job is to tell the story as it begs to be told. Neither embellish nor demean the work your youngsters did. They worked hard, learned a lot, and acquitted themselves well. Now show the public just how well they did!

Activity #39

Museology is just another facet of archaeology. First you recover the data, then you interpret and record your findings, and finally you put your specimens out for others to appreciate and enjoy. Remember, imagination is a major asset for any archaeologist.

Activities #40 & #41

CREATE A MUSEUM DISPLAY:
ACTIVITIES

ACTIVITY NO. 38

Activity:	Building a Diorama
Subjects:	Art, Language Arts, Science, Social Studies
Rationale:	This activity will acquaint the students with (1) setting up museum exhibits; and (2) making and using dioramas.
Objectives:	The students will build a diorama to showcase their archaeological site.

Activity Preparation:

☞ Explain *museology* and how the proper and imaginative display of artifacts and specimens enhances the public's interest in them.

☞ If you have taken a trip to a local museum, discuss with the students some of the things you have learned. Ask which *exhibits* stuck most in their minds. Why? Which exhibits, if any, were boring? Why?

☞ Discuss *dioramas*. Explain how they work. Discuss what kinds of dioramas would be effective for displaying the work done at the class site.

☞ Arrange to have space set aside in your school for your planned dioramas.

Activity:

☞ Separate the class into small museum teams (four at most).

☞ Have each team plan construction of a diorama covering some aspect of the site. Have each team make a sketch (with measurements) for review.

☞ Provide each team with the materials needed to build their diorama.

☞ Have the students choose the dioramas they want to use in their museum exhibit (or use them all).

☞ Add the artifacts and specimens and situate them for the public to enjoy. (Remember that you must have your exhibit in a place where people can view it but where your artifacts are safe.)

Materials Needed:

newspapers	papier mâché
white glue	poster board
construction paper	poster paints

Vocabulary:

museology	diorama
exhibit	

166

ACTIVITY NO. 39

Activity:	Building an Interpretive Exhibit
Subjects:	Art, Language Arts, Science, Social Studies
Rationale:	This activity will acquaint the students with setting up interpretive exhibits.
Objectives:	The students will construct an interpretive exhibit on some aspect of their site.

Activity Preparation:

☞ Review the role of *dioramas* with the class.

☞ Explain how museologists display artifacts and specimens in more informative ways than just labeling them on a shelf. With things you have on hand, demonstrate how to set up an *interpretive exhibit*. For example, show how you can demonstrate to the public how you repaired a pot or bottle. You may wish to include, as part of the exhibit, a duplication of your sandbox containing a bottle in the process of repair.

☞ Discuss with the class how the public is interested as much in what the students did as in what they recovered.

Activity:

☞ Divide the class into small teams.

☞ Have each team agree on one aspect of the dig project to do an exhibit on. [*Examples:* gridding the site, stringing it, excavating, note taking, repairing broken artifacts, labeling, etc.].

☞ Have each team showcase its completed exhibit in the classroom.

☞ Have the class members choose exhibits for public display (or use them all).

☞ Set up the exhibits in selected areas for public display.

Materials Needed:

newspaper	papier mâ ché
poster board	poster paints
markers	construction paper
pens and pencils	index cards

Vocabulary:

interpretive exhibits	dioramas

ACTIVITY NO. 40

Activity: Advertising an Event

Subjects: Art, Language Arts

Rationale: This activity will acquaint students with skills involved in designing a provocative ad.

Objectives: Students will design a full-color poster advertisement for their museum opening.

Activity Preparation:

☞ Bring in samples of magazine and newspaper *advertisements* for events like openings, exhibits, movies, and so forth. Explain their function, that is, to grab the public's interest. Explain what a *flyer* is. Show examples.

☞ Tell your students that you want them to design some effective and imaginative posters for their forthcoming museum displays. What would they include in their ad? Discuss.

Activity:

☞ Have each student design a flyer on 8½" x 11" colored paper.

☞ Post the flyers on the bulletin board and have the class decide which ones they wish to use for their museum opening. (Make some copies and distribute.)

☞ Divide the class into teams and give each team a full-size poster board and directions to create a poster ad. Tell your students that their ads will be judged for originality, color, and information content.

☞ Put the large posters in various areas around the school in advance of the exhibit.

☞ Award ribbons to the top three posters (blue, red, white) and attach to the winning posters.

Materials Needed:
poster boards
poster paints
8½" x 11" colored paper
colored markers
ribbons

Vocabulary:
advertisements
flyers

ACTIVITY NO. 41

Activity:	Prepare a Press Release
Subjects:	Language Arts
Rationale:	This activity will help students to understand the effectiveness of persuasive writing.
Objectives:	The students will prepare a press release announcing their museum opening.

Activity Preparation:

☞ Describe a *press release.* Explain how a good press release will entice *media* representatives to attend a function. Explain how press releases must be informative but, at the same time, interesting and provocative. Discuss ways that you can make something interesting to the media.

☞ If possible, have a representative from your local TV station or newspaper come by and talk to your class about the things they look for in a story.

Activity:

☞ Have each student write a press release for the forthcoming museum display.

☞ Let the class decide which media representatives they wish to send press releases.

☞ With a cover letter from the teacher, send the packet of press releases to the media.

☞ Results are guaranteed!

Materials Needed: pens or pencils
writing paper

Vocabulary: press release
media

TAKING THE SHOW ON THE ROAD

Sharing one's successes with others is a special thrill. Devise a way in which students can give a presentation or an illustrated lecture to other classes or groups. Speaking knowledgeably in front of groups will develop the self-confidence of the young archaeologists, and showing slides of the excavation, passing around and explaining the artifacts, and answering questions will hone communication skills.

Start by sharing your discoveries with your peers at school. Have the young archaeologists give slide lectures to kids in other classes that did not have the same field experience. After they've had the opportunity to tell their story to their schoolmates, move off the school grounds. Visit other elementary and secondary schools with your presentation. You'll be surprised how popular your traveling show will become. Just imagine what it can to do enhance a youngster's self-confidence and public-speaking skills. [**Note:** Schools uniformly love—and need—good public relations, and this is public relations at its best!]

Suitcase Museums

Most museums have a small traveling exhibit they send out to local schools. They call this their "suitcase museum" because it consists of a variety of artifacts, photographs, specimens, and so forth, which fit into a compartmentalized suitcase or small trunk. You can easily do the same thing with your site material. Convert an old suitcase or similar container into a handy carrier and fill it with a representative sampling of your finds—artifacts, specimens, drawings, photographs, or whatever you see fit to include—and you are on your way.

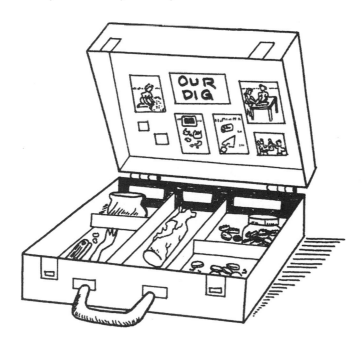

☞ Activity #42 ☜

Put on a TV Show

Youngsters are born actors. They love performing in front of people. You have the rare opportunity to exploit this natural inclination in concert with their newly completed archaeological project. Tell your students that a mock TV news or panel show is a good way to spread the information about their dig and the work they did. You will be pushing all of the right buttons.

☞ Activity #43 ☜

TAKING
THE SHOW
ON THE ROAD:
ACTIVITIES

ACTIVITY NO. 42

Activity:	A Suitcase Museum
Subjects:	Art, Language Arts, Science
Rationale:	This activity will help students understand what goes into the creation of a successful traveling exhibit.
Objectives:	The students will construct a suitcase museum.

Activity Preparation:

☞ If you have a local museum or historical society with a traveling exhibit, invite them to visit your class. If not, explain the concept of the suitcase museum. Explain how *suitcase museums* can get out to people who cannot get to a museum.

☞ Go over the kinds of material you would include in a suitcase museum of your site. Remind your students that space is a prime factor and that they must be selective in choosing what goes in. Relate the process to the creation of a *time capsule.*

☞ On the chalkboard, draw a suitcase museum, showing its various compartments, drawers, shelves, and so forth.

☞ Bring in an old, large suitcase (or small trunk) that you no longer need, or ask the class members if any of them has such an item.

Activity:

☞ Have the students make a list of things to include in the suitcase (again, reminding them of the limited space factor). Discuss the whys of each choice.

☞ Direct the students in physically converting the suitcase into a traveling museum.

☞ When the interior is finished, have the class decorate the exterior appropriately.

☞ Put together the traveling museum and send it "on the road." Start by having students take it to other classrooms in the school.

Materials Needed:

suitcase	duct tape
cardboard	boxes
miscellaneous construction materials	

Vocabulary:

suitcase museum	time capsule

ACTIVITY NO. 43

Activity: TV News Show

Subjects: Language Arts, Art, Science, Social Studies

Rationale: This activity will allow students to review information accumulated during the archaeological dig.

Objectives: The students will produce a TV news show about their archaeological dig.

Activity Preparation:
☞ Discuss with the students how news shows help inform the public.
☞ Review the dig project and elicit opinions as to what parts of the project were the most interesting. Which would make the best "news" stories?

Activity:
☞ Direct the class to write and produce a TV news show similar in format to the six o'clock news.
☞ Select (or have the class elect) co-anchors—one male, one female.
☞ Have class members assume the roles of field reporters, various experts, people being interviewed, and so forth.
☞ Have students decide on the station call letters, logo, and so forth and build a set that represents the six o'clock news desk.
☞ Direct students to write scripts for the various roles.
☞ Put on the news broadcast for the school.

Materials Needed: construction materials
props

APPENDIX A
TEACHER RESOURCES IN ARCHAEOLOGY

BOOKS FOR TEACHERS OF ARCHAEOLOGY

Joukowsky, M. (1980a). *Complete manual of field archaeology: Tools and techniques of field work for archaeologists.* Englewood Cliffs, NJ: Prentice-Hall.

McMillon, W. (1991). *The archaeology handbook: A field manual and resource guide.* New York: John Wiley.

BOOKS FOR STUDENTS OF ARCHAEOLOGY

Anderson, J. (1988). *From map to museum: Uncovering mysteries of the past.* New York: William Morrow.

Brennan, L. A. (1964). *The buried treasure of archaeology.* New York: Random House.

Brennan, L. A. (1973). *Beginners guide to archaeology.* Harrisburg, PA: Stackpole Books.

Cork, B. (1985). *Archaeology.* Tulsa: EDC Publishing.

Fradin, D. (1983). *Archaeology.* New York: Children's Press.

Hackwell, W. J. (1986). *Digging to the past: Excavations in ancient lands.* New York: Scribners.

Hackwell, W. J. (1988). *Diving to the past: Recovering ancient wrecks.* New York: Scribners.

Marston, E. (1986). *Mysteries in American archaeology.* New York: Walker.

McGovern, A. (1969). *If you lived in colonial times.* New York: Scholastic Books.

McNeil, M. J. & King, C. (1975). *How things began.* London: Usborne Publishing Ltd.

Merriman N. (1989). *Early humans.* New York: Knopf Books for Young Readers.

Morrison, V. F. (1981). *Going on a dig.* New York: Dodd, Mead.

National Geographic Society. (1976). *Clues to America's past.* Washington, DC: National Geographic Society.

Nichols, P. & Nichols, B. (1988). *Archaeology: The study of the past.* Austin, TX: Eakin-Sunbelt.

Oleksy, W. (1981). *Treasures of the land.* New York: Simon and Schuster.

Pickering, R. B. (1987). *I can be an archaeologist.* Chicago: Children's Press.

Porell, B. (1979). *Digging the past: Archaeology in your own backyard.* Reading, ME: Addison-Wesley.

Sauvin, P. (1985). *Do you know how history began?* New York: Warwick Press.

Snyder, T. F. (1982). *Archaeology search book.* New York: McGraw-Hill.

Wong, O. K. (1988). *Prehistoric people.* Chicago: Children's Press.

ARTICLES FOR TEACHERS OF ARCHAEOLOGY

Carroll, R. F. (1987). Schoolyard archaeology. *The Social Studies, 78*(2), 67–75.

Catalina, L. J. (1983). Digging into hometown. *Cobblestone Magazine, 4*(6), 10–13.

Cotter, J. L. (1979). Archaeologists of the future: High schools discover archaeology. *Archaeology, 32*(1), 29–35.

Passe, J. & Passe, M. (1985) Archaeology: A unit to promote thinking skills. *The Social Studies, 76*(6), 238–239.

Watts, L. E. (1985). They dig archaeology. *Science and Children, 23* (9), 5–9.

Welsh, C. L. (1994). Digging through history. *Gifted Child Today, 17*(1), 18–20, 42.

White, J. R. (1976). Field archaeology in the high school curriculum. *American Secondary Education, 7*(1), 3–7.

White, J. R. (1992). Fake mound, genuine scholarship: An exercise in field archaeology for the gifted. *Gifted Child Today, 15*(5), 2–6.

White J. R. (1995). Empty lots as modern classrooms. *Gifted Child Today, 18*(5), 12–16, 42.

McCann, A. M. (1991). High-tech linkup for kids. *Archaeology, 44*(1), 44–46.

Shade, R. (1990). Grandma's attic: Bringing archaeology closer to home for the G/C/T student. *Gifted Child Today, 13*(3), 10–12.

Smith, K. C. (1991). At last, a meeting of the minds. *Archaeology, 44*(1), 36–39.

TEACHING MATERIALS, GUIDES, ACTIVITIES

Calduto, M. J., & Bruhac, J. (1989). *Keepers of the Earth: Native American stories and environmental activities for children.* Golden, CO: Fulcrum.

Calduto, M. J. & Bruhac, J. (1991). *Keepers of the animals: Native American stories and wildlife activities for children.* Golden, CO: Fulcrum.

Cork, B., & Reid, S. (1987). *The young scientist book of archaeology: Discovery of the past with science and technology.* Tulsa: EDC Publishing.

Cultural Heritage Education Team. (1993). *Intrigue of the past, investigating archaeology.* Delores, CO: Cultural Heritage Education Team: Anasazi Heritage Center. [Address: Anasazi Heritage Center 27501 Highway 91, Delores, CO 81323.]

Dickens, R., & McKinley, J. (1979). *Frontiers in the Soil.* Frontiers Publishing: Atlanta.

Doherty, E. (1981). *Stones and bones: Archaeology.* East Windsor Hill, CT: Synergetics. [Address: Synergetics, Box 84, East Windsor Hill, CT 06028.]

Harrison, M. (1984). *Archaeology: Walney.* Fairfax, VA: Fairfax County Park Authority. [Address: Museum Education Coordinator, County Park Authority, 3701 Pender Drive, Fairfax, VA 22030.]

Hawkins, N. (1984). *Classroom archaeology.* Baton Rouge, LA: Division of Archaeology: Baton Rouge. [Address: Division of Archaeology, Office of Cultural Development, State of Louisiana, P.O. Box 44247, Baton Rouge, LA 70804.]

Lattimore, D. (1986). *Digging into the past.* Dominguez Hillls, CA: Educational Insights.

McNutt, N. (1988). *Project archaeology: Saving traditions.* Longmont, CO: Sopris West. [Address: Sopris West Inc., 1120 Delaware Avenue, Longmont, CO 80501.]

National Council for Social Studies. (1991). *Classroom sources for archaeology education.* Washington, DC: National Park Service.

National Trust for Historic Preservation. (1990). *Everything we know about archaeology for you to use in your classroom: A workshop for teachers.* Washington, DC: National Park Service.

Neuman, R. (1983). *Sleuthing through history: An introduction to archaeology.* Portland, ME: J. Weston Walch.

Pena, E. (1989). *Archaeology activity pack.* Waterford, NY: New York State Bureau of Historic Sites. [Address: Bureau of Historic Sites, Peebles Island, Waterford, NY 12188.]

Price, T. D. & Gebauer, A. (1996). *Adventures in Fugawiland: A computer simulation in archaeology.* Mountain View, CA: Mayfield: Mountain View.

Sanders, K. K. (1986). *Archaeology is more than a dig.* Tucson, AZ: Tucson Unified School District.

Smith, K. C. & McManamon, F. (1991). *Archaeology and education: The classroom and beyond.* Washington, DC: Archaeological Assistance Study, No. 2, National Park Service.

Suffolk County Archaeological Association. *Native life and archaeology workbook.* Stony Brook, NY: Suffolk County Archaeological Association. [Address: Suffolk County Archaeological Association, P.O. Drawer AR, Stony Brook, NY 11790.]

Wheat, P., & Wharton, B. (1990). *Clues from the past: A resource book on archaeology.* Dallas: Hendrick-Long.

GAMES, KITS, AND SIMULATION MODELS

Mummy's Message
A simulation game about an archaeological expedition to Egypt (grades 5–12).
Interact
P.O. Box 997-S89
Lakeside, CA 92040

Time Capsule
An interactive unit focusing on preservation of the American culture (grades 5–12).
Interact

Dig 2
A simulation game on reconstructing a past civilization (grades 5–8).
Interact

Miscellaneous Kits
Unearth and restore replicas of artifacts from various Old World sites. Ask for catalog.
Archaeological Institute of America
675 Commonwealth Avenue
Dept. C1
Boston, MA 02215-1401

FILMS AND SLIDES

SLIDES

The Archaeological Institute of America has an extensive collection of slides covering various aspects of archaeological work. Write to them for a catalog at:

Archaeological Institute of America, Long Island Society
Great Neck Library
Bayview Avenue and Grist Mill Lane
Great Neck, NY 11024

FILMS

Most of the *films* or *videos* listed below are available for rental at reasonable prices from:

Penn State Audio-Visual Services
The Pennsylvania State University
Special Services Building
1127 Fox Hill Road
University Park, PA
Write to them for a free *annotated* catalog of their audio-visual resources.

- *Archaeologists At Work* (1962) 16mm Film, Video, (14 min.)
Shows archaeologists in the act of digging, sifting, and testing. Discussion of methods and theory of archaeology.(grades 6–12)
- *The Big Dig For Little People* (1976) 16mm Film (15 min.)
Excavation of a Philistine house in Israel. Uses question/answer format. (grades 1–9)
- *Other People's Garbage* (1980) Video (59 min.)
Review of three archaeological projects in the U.S. What do artifacts tell us about earlier lifestyles? (grades 10–12) (one of the Odyssey Series)
- *Search for a Century* (1980) 16mm Film, Video (59 min.)
Excavations at Wolstoneholme Towne, a seventeenth-century settlement in Virginia. (grades 7–12)
- *Dig* (1972) 16mm Film (25 min.)
An animated musical in which a rock explains what stratigraphy is to a boy and his dog as they travel to the Earth's center. (grades 4–6)
- *How Man Discovers His Past* (1970) 16mm Film, Video (20 min.)
Shows how human history is being constantly re-interpreted as new evidence is brought to light. (grades 7–12)
- *The Williamsburg File* (1976) 16mm Film, Video (45 min.)
The archaeology involved in the restoration of Colonial Williamsburg, Virginia. (grades 10–12)
- *Seeking the First Americans* (1980) 16mm Film, Video (59 min.)
Archaeological theories about the arrival of the first people to reach the New World between 12,000 and 50,000 years ago. (grades 10–12)
- *The Case of the Ancient Astronauts* (1979) 16mm Film, Video (57 min.)
Debunking the scientific inadequacy of the theories of Erich Von Daniken's "Chariot of the Gods." (grades 10–12)

MISCELLANEOUS SOURCES

The following references are for sources which should be of great value to teachers interested in undertaking an archaeological unit of the sort described in this book.

AnthroNotes: National Museum of Natural History Bulletin for Teachers
This booklet is published three times a year (Fall, Winter, and Spring) and is an extremely informative publication for teachers, featuring a wide variety of anthropological topics including much on archaeology. The bulletin with its illustrations and activities may be reproduced and distributed free-of-charge for educational purposes. This bulletin is free to teachers who may be added to the mailing list by writing:

P. Ann Kaupp
Anthropology Outreach and Public Information Office
Department of Anthropology
NHB 363 MRC 112
Smithsonian Institution
Washington, D.C. 20560

Archaeology and Education
This biannual newsletter is devoted to diverse issues of interest to teachers. Interesting ideas for activities and valuable lesson materials are included. For a subscription write to:

Archaeological Resource Center
Danforth Technical School
840 Greenwood Avenue
Toronto, Ontario Canada

Archaeologists of the Americas. This is a complete membership directory listing all professional archaeologists who are members of the Society for American Archaeology. Included are addresses, phone numbers, and e-mail addresses. A special price of $30.00 gets this directory plus *Archaeology and Public Education* (see above). [**Note:** You really only need to get this directory once; after that, switch back to the $10.00 per year bulletin.] To purchase, write to the SAA address (under Number 2, above).

APPENDIX B
ARCHAEOLOGICAL FORMS

HISTORIC ARTIFACT DISCARD SHEET

SITE _____   F.S. NO. _____

Location_____

Depth _____

Description	Quantity	Comment
1.		
2.		
3.		
4.		
5.		
6.		
7.		
8.		
9.		
10.		
11.		
12.		
13.		
14.		
15.		
16.		
17.		
18.		
19.		
20.		
21.		
22.		
23.		
24.		
25.		

Date_____   Recorder _____

GENERAL FEATURE FORM

Feature No. _____   Site _____

Square No. _____   County _____

1. Definition_____
_____
_____

2. Location

    Horizonal _____

    _____

    Depth _____

3. Dimensions

    Date _____

    a. Max. Length_____   Direction _____

    b. Max. Width _____   Direction _____

    c. Vertical Thickness _____

4. Fill _____
_____
_____

5. Preservation _____

6. Associations

    a. Features _____   b. Specimens _____

    _____   _____

    _____   _____

    _____   _____

    _____   _____

7. Comments _____
_____
_____
_____
_____

Date_____   Recorder _____

ARTIFACT DATA SHEET

1. Depth_____ in.; _____ cm.

2. Location in Unit:

    S of NW corner _____ in.; _____ cm.

    E of NW corner _____ in.; _____ cm.

3. Map of Location

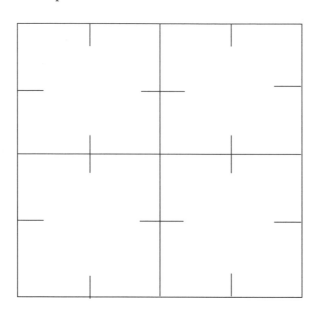

4. Scale _____ 5' x 5' _____ 10' x 10' _____Meter

5. Sketch

SITE _____

UNIT _____

6. Artifact Description _____

_____

_____

_____

_____

7. Associations _____

_____

_____

_____

_____

_____

8. Preservation or Speical Care_

_____

_____

_____

_____

9. Remarks _____

_____

_____

_____

_____

_____

Date _____ Recorder _____

UNIVERSAL DATA FORM

_____ FORM SITE _____ UNIT _____

1. Definition: _____

_____

_____

_____

_____

2. Associations: _____

_____

_____

3.

Scale:

Legend:

4. Observations: _____

_____

_____

Date _____ Recorder _____

CONTINUATION SHEET

page _____

_____ FORM   SITE _____ UNIT _____

Date _____   Recorder _____

PHOTO LOG

Date	Roll #	Type (BW or Color)	Subject and Description	Site	Neg #	Photo-grapher

ACCESSION LOG

Date	FS No.	Location	Depth	Item No.	Description

SITE FORM

1. Site Number	4. Site Name
2.County	5. Other Names for Site
3. Township	

6. City or Town Vicinity of _	12. Land Form	20. Ownership: Public
7. Map Reference	13. Elevation	Private
	14. Soil Type	21. Form Prepared by
8. Township and Range Number	15. Floral Cover	
9. Section Number	16. Condition of Site	22. Organization:
10. U.T.M. Reference	17. Present Use	
☐☐ ☐☐☐☐☐☐ ☐☐☐☐☐☐	18. Type of Site	23. Date of Survey
Zone Easting Northing	19. Dimensions of Site	24. Survey Conditions
11. Verbal Site Location		25. Cultural Classification or Time Period

26. Artifacts Collected

27. References

28. Use opposite side to copy portions of topographic map with site located, attachment of contact print, sketch of site plan, or continuation of itens 1–32.

UNIT LEVEL RECORD

NW

SITE _____

UNIT _____

Depth _____ to _____ cm.

Soil Texture

_____

Artifact Key

1. _____
2. _____
3. _____
4. _____
5. _____
6. _____
7. _____
8. _____
9. _____
10. _____
11. _____
12. _____
13. _____
14. _____
15. _____

(list additional artifacts on reverse side)

Feature Key

Description of Features:

_____

_____

_____

_____

Comments and Interpretations:

_____

_____

_____

_____

Date _____ Recorder _____